Are You Ready!

Are You Ready!

Take Charge,

Lose Weight,

Get in Shape,

and

Change Your Life Forever

HACHETTE AUSTRALIA

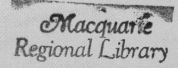

HACHETTE AUSTRALIA

Published in Australia and New Zealand in 2008
by Hachette Australia
(An imprint of Hachette Livre Australia Pty Limited)
Level 17, 207 Kent Street, Sydney NSW 2000
Website: www.hachette.com.au

Offset by arrangement with Broadway Books, an imprint of The Doubleday Broadway Publishing Group, a division of Random House, Inc., New York.

Cataloguing-in-Publication data
available from the National Library of Australia

Book design by Ralph Fowler / rlf design
Photographs by Ryan Forbes Photography
Cover adaptation by Kinart
Internal adaptation by Bookhouse, Sydney
Printed in Australia by Griffin Press, Adelaide

Hachette Livre Australia's policy is to use papers that are natural, renewable and recyclable products and made from wood grown in sustainable forests. The logging and manufacturing processes are expected to conform to the environmental regulations of the country of origin.

I dedicate this book to all of my Blue Teams from The Biggest Loser.

Without all of you, this book would not have been possible.

Working with each and every one of you has made me

the compassionate trainer that I am today—thank you.

You all are my inspiration.

Testimonials

"Words cannot express what Bob Harper means to me. He has been not only my trainer but my motivator, my mentor, my confidante, and friend! He gave me the confidence to go from a former 'Biggest Loser' to competing as Mrs. Tennessee-United States in the Mrs. United States competition. He inspires me to be a better person both inwardly and outwardly. Bob Harper is one in a million. He is quite treasured and deeply loved!"

—Ryan Kelley

"This book gives people a chance to bring Bob home. I was so blessed to have been chosen by Bob to work with him on a daily basis. People often remind me how lucky I was to spend those precious, LONG days with Bob, and they're right. But now they too have that chance with this book. Read and really listen to this man: he will change your life like he changed mine. He actually saved my life! Bob is a true giver of himself, a rare and genuine human being. Thanks for stopping this train from going over the cliff. I am so fortunate to be the recipient of the gift of you, and so proud that your book will do the same for millions. I love you Bob!"

—Erik Chopin, Season 3's Winner of *The Biggest Loser*

"For someone who has been overweight his whole life, I have often been consumed by a sense of hopelessness when it comes to weight loss. Being diagnosed with health problems in my early twenties, it was easy for me to neglect my heath risks for the long term. Bob Harper has truly been the answer to all my prayers! He stands as a sign of hope and inspiration for so many people that has forever put me on the path of defeating my struggles with obesity! His knowledge, experience, and outright will to change people's lives is the real solution to the world's struggle with being overweight. Bob's influence on my life (from NBC's *The Biggest Loser*) has shown me the power a person possesses to overcome any obstacle. He has not just come in to my life as a trainer, but I'm happy to say he has become a life-long friend who has shown me that the human spirit of will and determination can conquer anything! Bob taught me the mentality of acknowledging that I deserve a happy and healthy lifestyle. With his help, I was able to lose over

200 lbs without the need of weight loss surgery. I'm proud to say that I have refused to let the obesity epidemic control my life anymore. So *Are You Ready* to change your life? Bob Harper has forever changed mine!"

—Neil Tejwani

"Coming from someone who has been overweight their entire life, getting ready to make a change is hard, but more importantly, it's scary. Before I met Bob I thought my life was set and that I would always be overweight. I thought I would always be that fat girl who yearned to be thin. I always thought I was ready, and I tried to be ready numerous times, but only met failure. Bob showed me there is no other time than now. His passion and knowledge about health and fitness helped me become the person I always wanted to be. To try and put into words what Bob has done for me is nearly impossible. His commitment to me and my well being has completely changed my life. The ability he has to transform not only your body but also your mind is what sets him apart from the rest. He singlehandedly made *The Biggest Loser* experience for me with his love, dedication, and amazing sense of humor. Any person who comes into Bob's life is blessed and I am not only proud to call him my trainer, but also my friend. There is no other time than now to begin your life, and there is no other person than Bob Harper to get you started. Bob showed me it CAN be done. So get ready; you won't believe what you've been missing."

—Nicole Michalik
GO BLUE! ☺

"Three years ago I had an opportunity to change my life. Not only by going on *The Biggest Loser,* but getting to work with Bob. Bob not only gave me the tools to achieve my goals, but gave me the reasons why. He helped me to realize that if I dont put time into me, I won't be able to helps others. He pushed me to do things I never knew or thought I could do. With his encouragement and confidence in me, I gained confidence in myself. He saw what I didn't and taught me to see it in me. Just having had a baby, I am using these same principals to take off the baby weight. Every morning when I am at the gym I remind myself that I have to take time for me and put myself first so I can be better for my son. Thank you, Bob, for giving me the tools to be a better me!"

—Suzy Hoover

Contents

Acknowledgments

The writing of a book is never a solitary project. So many wonderful and important people have encouraged and helped me make my book a reality. I would like to thank Ellen DeGeneres—you made me think outside the box and push myself to my fullest potential. You taught me that anything is possible.

I am eternally grateful for the sage advice and constant direction of my agent, Brett Hansen. Also I would like to acknowledge Peter Steinberg, my literary agent whose wise counsel led me both to Stacy Creamer, my wonderful, thoughtful editor at Broadway Books, and to Billie Fitzpatrick, my collaborator, who understood me and put my heart and soul into this book.

A big heartfelt thank-you to Mark Koops, who has been a constant ear and support to me every day of our working career: No matter what, you always make time for me. Thanks also to J.D. Roth and Dave Broome, for seeing something in me and allowing me to do what I so love to do. Thanks, too, to Francois Moebasser and Mark Murphy, the brothers I never had.

I would also like to acknowledge two very important people in my life. First, Cristi Conaway: You keep me constantly grounded and gave me the best gift of my life, a family. You opened your heart and your house to me and welcomed me with open arms. Without you, my life would be less. You are my heart. . . .

And to my best friend, Kate Angelo: You saw something in me at a time when I could not see it. You are the best friend that anyone could ever ask for. Your unconditional love has given me a stronger foundation in my own life. You are simply fantastic.

I would also like to acknowledge Patty and Ashby Grantham, the parents I always wanted. Also, my very close friends Darren Gold, Brian Tatara, Marilyn Howard, Wendy Lusby, Lynne Scholer. My godchildren, Coco and Miles. My friends at Reveille, 3 Ball Productions and the rest of my *Biggest Loser* family.

I extend special thanks to my sister Debbie Johnson, my eternal touchstone, and to the memory of my mother: I love you.

God is Love.

Are
You
Ready!

Measurements in this book are in US pounds and inches. Please refer to the table below for conversions to Australian metric measurements.

1 pound = 0.45 kilogram

5 pounds = 2.26 kilograms

10 pounds = 4.5 kilograms

20 pounds = 9 kilograms

100 pounds = 45.35 kilograms

1 inch = 2.54 centimetres

5 inches = 12.7 centimetres

1 foot = 30.48 centimetres

5 foot = 152.4 centimetres

Introduction

Y ou are about to take charge of your life, and I am here to give you the inspiration, the encouragement, and the tools to make it happen! The book that you now hold in your hands is the result of more than fifteen years of my passionate mission: to help people get in the best shape possible through an eating and fitness plan that will rewire your brain and reconnect you to your heart so that you never have to diet again. This is my promise to you.

Over the years I have had numerous opportunities to work with many Hollywood stars as well as—and perhaps more important—the everyday women and men, fathers and mothers, who had hundreds of pounds to lose on the hit TV show *The Biggest Loser*. And now I would like to share all of what I do with you—the millions of viewers of the show and the many of you who write to me and call me.

Over the past twenty years, as I have been crystallizing my approach to diet and fitness, two things have become clear to me: (1) When I work with clients in person, I am able to unlock an essential key that enables them to understand fitness from the inside out, which is a key that guarantees their success; and (2) no plan out there, whether offered by personal trainers or books, has quite figured out the combination to this lock before now. In *Are You Ready!* I offer this key that gets to the root of your ability to love, respect, and cherish your body. When this transformation happens, the eating and fitness plan are simple, straightforward, and successful. Just wait and see.

Are You Ready! takes all of what I do with clients in person and delivers it in a form that you can truly make your own, on your own. Of course, this book offers a carefully strategized dietary and fitness program, one that is easy to follow and easy to stick to. You will be able to lose weight, whether the ten stubborn pounds that have lingered since childbirth or the one hundred pounds that have slowly but surely crept onto your body, taking hold of your entire existence. My cutting-edge fitness plan will enhance your weight loss and hone your body so your silhouette becomes toned, strong, and naturally suited to your physique.

I've witnessed thousands of people lose tens of thousands of pounds utilizing my eating and fitness plan, but the most powerful feature to my approach, the one that separates it from all the other programs, promises, and plans out there, is the Inner Compass. What is the Inner Compass? It's the mental and emotional dimension of my plan, the key that unlocks how you can once and for all take charge of your body, your mind, and your life so you can find true health, happiness, and peace. For I believe that these three great blessings—health, happiness, and peace—go together and can be achieved together, and are really what is at the root of learning how to take care of ourselves.

Are You Ready! is not only my own personal story of how I got to be where I am today but also the cumulative result of honing and perfecting my one-on-one work with hundreds of women and men over a fifteen-year span. So before I share with you the details of my Inner Compass plan, let me take you a few years back (well, maybe more than a few, but who's counting?) to when it all began.

I was living in Nashville, Tennessee, in a one-bedroom apartment that was right beside a small gym. I was new to the big city, having grown up on a farm miles from any town, and was trying to figure out what to do with my life. I often watched people walking into the gym stressed and frazzled from their day only to emerge an hour or so later much, much happier. I could literally see a glow on their faces and an almost visible bounce in their step. Something had obviously happened in there, and I figured they had a secret, a secret I wanted to know about. After a few weeks of contemplation, I summoned my courage and walked through the door of the gym. I remember feeling intimidated by all those hard, muscular, fit bodies, but I signed up for an aerobics class (I told you, it was the 1980s) from a teacher who looked like Jamie Lee Curtis in *Perfect* but who acted like Rambo. She kicked my ass—and I wanted more. I loved the high I got after a fierce workout. I loved the way my body began to feel strong and agile. I loved the way becoming fit made my confidence grow and my aspirations take shape.

I became a regular at the gym, and soon the owner approached me and suggested that I would make a great trainer and instructor. I was stunned. I was also inspired. She saw something in me, the way I connected with people and made them feel at ease. One of the first pieces of advice she gave me was to remember that training people and teaching them about fitness was all about making clients feel good about themselves. I got it. I understood this immediately and instinctively: It was the inside—the heart and the mind—that needed to be awakened in order for someone to really commit to taking care of their bodies. And it was this first connection—how the mind and heart speak to the body—that became the cornerstone of how I train people to fully utilize diet and fitness to become the best people they can be.

With this inspiration, I began to develop a program that gets to the center of people's motivation, the place that nine times out of ten stops people from truly being successful at getting fit, losing weight, and keeping it off in a healthy way. Sure, a lot of people can diet for six weeks, six months, sometimes even a year. They can begin a workout program, see visible results, and actually admire what stares back at them from the mirror. But the more I worked with people, the more I realized that unless I first addressed what I call the Inner Compass, that place within someone that houses the person *not* visible in the mirror, they would always fall off the wagon, gain back the weight, and, most frustrating of all, never really understand why, yet again, they hadn't succeeded.

Armed with this insight and an even greater sense of destiny, I realized that if I was really going to make the best possible career out of fitness, I would need to move to the fitness capital of the world—Los Angeles, California. I packed my Toyota Corolla to the gills, drove from my longtime home in Tennessee, and headed West, resolving to quiet the fears that were rumbling in the pit of my stomach.

Now, more than fifteen years later, I have trained some of Hollywood's biggest stars. I have helped them make beautiful bodies more beautiful, more slender, and more fit. But it wasn't until my first day of shooting *The Biggest Loser* that I felt my true calling, deep in my bones. When I saw these big people coming down those stairs, I thought, *Do I have what it takes?* All of a sudden it was clear that I wasn't working with actors who were trying to transform their already toned abs into a six-pack or trying to go from a size six to a size two; I was working with people who wanted to be able to walk their daughters down the aisle. I was working with parents who wanted to be around so they could see their kids have kids. Basically, I was working with people who wanted another chance at life—the stakes were high, and the odds against them were higher.

These participants from *The Biggest Loser* were from all across America, and their lives were ruled by their weight. They had spent most of their adult lives trying dozens of diets, and nothing had ever truly worked. They had been crushed by failure heaped upon failure. And now they were going to be on a television show trying to lose weight in front of millions of television viewers. It seemed impossible, and it was my job to make it happen!

As I began working with the *Biggest Loser* participants, I soon realized that I was going to have to take my work as a trainer to whole different level. If I were going to help these women and men lose weight and get in shape, I had to rewire their mind-heart circuitry at a deep enough level that they would never relapse again. I also realized that I had to practice what I preach, and start with my own head and heart. This is when I had an exciting insight into another dimension of my Inner Compass plan.

It's one thing to teach and another thing entirely to do. I wanted to be a role model, and that meant living the life that these people were aspiring to achieve. I wasn't going to show people one way and have me live another. Was I out of shape? No. Did I need to lose weight? No. Did I need to connect to my own Inner Compass, that part of me that spoke the truth about how best to take care of myself? Yes.

So the first thing I did was begin keeping a food journal. When I paid this level of attention to what I ate, when I wrote down on the page everything I put in my mouth, it became easier to see and then understand my relationship with food and how it affected my day-to-day life. Yes, I had been a trainer for many years and ate a well-balanced diet, but I soon discovered that, like most people, I use food emotionally. I saw that I would reach for food in times of stress, when I had any negative feeling about myself, or when I was feeling overwhelmed by the daily challenges of life. Instead of feeling my feelings, I ate my feelings. Granted, I wasn't overeating or binge-eating. But still, I was using food to compensate for emotional issues that I wasn't willing to deal with, which is exactly what anyone who struggles with weight does. As I began observing and working with the *Biggest Loser* participants, I realized that their emotional eating was so out of control that they no longer knew *why* they reached for food, and they couldn't stop when they did. Keeping my food journal was one of the most important ways I reached this new understanding of how I could help them stop this self-sabotage once and for all.

Every day, my major focus became trying to make the right choices. I created a game plan that was fueled by my knowledge about diet and nutrition, and I began planning my meals in advance. I also made sure to schedule a specific time for my workout, knowing I'd be more motivated to do it if I had an actual appointment with myself. Very quickly, I felt stronger during my workouts because I was now fueling my body properly. I also had more energy and less stress because I wasn't burning the candle at both ends. And I was getting enough good rest.

At about this time, I was in the midst of shooting the first season finale of *The Biggest Loser* in Australia when my mother had a fatal heart attack. It was Christmas Eve, and my mom had complained about a slight headache; then suddenly, within hours, my strong, invincible mother had been felled. I had never imagined before that my mother, of all people, could develop heart disease. At seventy years of age, my mother was mildly overweight, with an extra roll or two around her middle—a telltale sign, I was soon to learn, that she had a propensity for heart disease. And she had high blood pressure, but didn't everyone past the age of sixty-five? But looking back, it was her lifestyle that was the real reason behind her life coming to an end so drastically: She had never really taken care of herself, having eaten a diet high in dairy and meat fat and never truly exercising.

My mother's death, painful and heartbreaking as it was, actually triggered an epiphany: I came to the wide-eyed realization that we have to treat our bodies as sacred vessels, something to honor, cherish, and respect. When we treat our bodies with love and care, everything in our life becomes much, much more attainable. And when we don't, illness and dissatisfaction will be ours.

Cherishing your body and treating it with respect requires a shift in thinking, one in which you stop emotional eating and create an empowering relationship with food. It was this insight and understanding that led me to create the next dimension of my Inner Compass plan.

Most of us can be our own worst enemy. We beat ourselves up and call ourselves the worst names in the world as we go through the day. Just imagine for a second what that barrage of negativity can do to a person's sense of self-worth, self-esteem, and overall outlook on life. It can be quite grim. The proactive formula of my Inner Compass plan will get you to hear your internal tape recorder from a distance and then acknowledge the patterns or links between that tape recording and your negative behaviors. And eventually you can—and will—change your way of thinking. When you go from being your own worst enemy to your own best friend, not only will the weight fall off but your life will become more manageable, livable, and enjoyable. Suddenly you go from being a passenger in your own life to sitting in the driver's seat, with the entire landscape ahead of you. It is that sense of self-worth that I want to drive into your brain so that when you encounter stress, obstacles, or just plain weariness, you can fall back on these new, healthy habits of mind.

For years and years, I knew how to push my body to the limit. But that was just it—to the limit means without respect, without listening to my body, without truly knowing and loving my body. When I really started to respect my body, my body started taking care of me. This is the goal of *Are You Ready!* and its Inner Compass program—to show you how to listen to your body, learn to love and respect your body, so that your body, in turn, will take care of you.

Although I miss my mother every day of my life, I am forever grateful for the lesson I learned from her: She inspired me to treat my body with care, and perhaps more important, she inspired me to help others learn to treat their bodies with care. I want people to treat their bodies as sacred vessels because I know when this happens, all the years of false starts, yo-yo diets, bad voices in their heads telling them to eat or not to eat, whatever, will come to an end.

"Are you ready?" That's one of the most important questions I ask any new client. Until you are ready to make these lasting changes, there is nothing I can do. But when you are ready, I will move mountains to help you get what you want. When I work one-on-one with people, I help instill this personal self-respect, and after that seed has been planted in the soul, it will grow and grow. But it needs water, food, and lots and lots of love.

Indeed, my book is for anyone who struggles with getting back in charge of their life. This book can work for someone who wants to lose 10 pounds or for someone who needs to lose 200 pounds. Mostly this book is for the people out there who want to change a behavior that doesn't work for them anymore. This book is for the person who needs to find the true friend that lives in each and every one of us. This book is for anyone who has decided that *today* is the day that he can take charge of his life.

———————

Are You Ready! will not only guide you to lose weight and get into the best shape of your life but, most important of all, give you the tools to rewire your brain so that once and for all you understand your relationship with food, tap into tools that can change your self-sabotaging behaviors, and finally assert control over how and when you eat. This is what your Inner Compass is all about. When you begin your Inner Compass journey, in Part 1, you will come to a unique way of understanding what makes you tick, and cultivate the tools and know-how to reinvent your relationship with food. The Inner Compass plan offers a four-step strategy, including "Are You *Really* Ready?," "Accept Where You Are and Forgive," "Love Yourself," and "Change Your Internal Tape Recorder, Change Yourself." In each of the four steps, you will gain insight and practical strategies so you can overcome negative thought patterns and bad behaviors, and replace this old system with one that is self-empowering, self-loving, and self-motivating.

In Part 2, "Stepping Up to the Plate: Your Diet," you will then become familiar with my easy-to-follow eating plan, which is a simple, healthy way to help you lose weight. In the beginning you will be asked to do some calorie counting and portion control, recording what you eat and when you eat in your food journal. But in a matter of a few weeks, you will be so familiar with how much and what types of food to eat, you will be able to eyeball amounts and forget about counting those calories. You will have earned the right to make the best possible choices for yourself.

You will be eating plenty of whole foods that are nutrient dense, clean, and naturally low in calories and high in fiber. One of the keys to this plan is making sure to eat every four hours. This not only offsets hunger, but keeps you away from triggers that cause overeating or unnecessary snacking. Chapters include "It's an Eating Plan, Not a Diet," "Your Food Journal," and "Stress Busters." Of course, I've worked in creative food lists, tips on eating on the run and in restaurants, and ideas about how to navigate travel. You will see how to seamlessly integrate this eating plan into your life in a daily way, lose the weight you desire, and realize you never have to diet again.

Part 3 of the book focuses on my fitness plan, which requires minimal equipment, can be done anywhere, and suits any level of fitness. So whether you haven't lifted a leg in ten years or are already running 20 miles a week, this fitness program will strengthen you, tone you, and improve your cardiovascular health, which all maximize and enhance your weight loss. The fitness plan is broken down into two phases. In Phase One I ask everyone to begin with four weeks of pure cardio, which enables you to make exercise part of your routine and get your body moving, as you change the way you eat. At the end of this four-week period, you are ready, both physically and mentally, to start Phase Two, which adds circuit training and core challenges to strengthen your upper and lower body and core (the muscles of your abs and back that strengthen and stabilize your spine). The more familiar you become with the strength-training exercises, the more motivated you will be to expand your repertoire of individual workouts. The more fit you become, the more able and excited you will be to increase the intensity and duration of your workout.

Throughout Part 3, you will also find tips on how to make your workout part of your daily and/or weekly schedule. You'll feel inspired to stick with your new regime because you will have the confidence and commitment to do so. Taking all that you gained from your Inner Compass work, you will learn a completely new orientation to your body and how to work out so that you will never quit again. And when you see how much clarity of mind and focus you gain by working out, you will be *self*-motivated to find that time. It may be a cliché that exercise gives you energy, but it's true nonetheless. Exercising the body sharpens the mind, making you able to get more work done in less time.

So are you ready? You bet you are!

PART 1

Your Inner Compass

Getting started is always hard because it goes against everything you think you know about yourself and everything you count on as being familiar. As you begin your own Inner Compass journey, you will learn more about yourself than you ever thought possible. You will come to a new understanding about your relationship with food, gain insight into why you may be using food emotionally—eating your feelings instead of feeling your feelings—and you will learn to see how (and when) certain self-sabotaging behaviors are triggered by certain thoughts and feelings. With this knowledge of yourself, I will then guide you to shed the fear, the shame, and the old behaviors that have held you captive, so that once and for all you will feel liberated and free to seize the change you want.

In the next few chapters, you will delve deep into yourself. You may feel uncomfortable, you may even feel afraid. That's all good. Uprooting any kind of ingrained behaviors and deep feelings always stirs everything up, which is why it becomes crucial to keep yourself focused on your overarching goal: to lose weight, get in shape, and be the best person you can be.

During periods of change, some people rely on blind faith in a higher power; others find that power within themselves. Some people use a bit of both. When I first got into my old Toyota Corolla and headed west toward Los Angeles, leaving all that was familiar behind, I prayed the whole way in order to help move through my fear of the unknown. Getting past this fear is what you will be doing as you learn to take charge of your life. But remember, you won't be alone—you will have me and this book as your guides. So hold on tight, and keep this in mind: You can do it, and you will!

ONE

Are You *Really* Ready?

— Step One —

I am going to help you get inside of yourself to that place that has been the root of all your weight challenges. Have you tried two, ten, or twenty diets over the years? Have you lost weight and put it back on? Have you tried and tried to change the way you eat, but to no avail? Do you still feel that food is controlling you instead of the other way around?

If any of these questions resonate with you, then know that you are in the right place. You are not going to get a lot of medical jargon out of me, but what you will get is a man who has lived what you will find in this book—a man who believes every word that you will read here and who has gotten thousands of pounds off a nation with my technique.

When you begin this diet and fitness program, especially its Inner Compass plan, you will be receiving from me not false encouragement or empty promises but advice directly from my heart. Many diet gurus and fitness coaches are "head thinkers." Not me. I am a "heart thinker." And that's where I begin, connecting with your heart. Why? Because I know that you have been down this road before. You know the good foods from the bad, the way to lose weight, and why exercise is so good for you. But what has not happened before is making that connection between your heart and your head. And that's exactly what the Inner Compass plan will help you accomplish: reconnect your heart and mind so that you will never have to go on another diet!

So let's start at the beginning with one question: Are you ready? *Really* ready to change your life?

Turning Points

This question may seem simple, but take a moment to consider what it takes for you to stand on the precipice of change and truly take responsibility to make that change. For my client Taylor, age 33, it was a health report. For years he ignored his rising weight. Then, on his last physical exam, his doctor told him he had developed type 2 diabetes. Suddenly, Taylor saw his life flash before his eyes and he decided he had to do something or he was literally going to die.

Many people I have worked with over the years have been forced to confront a health scare in order to get them to pay attention to what they need to change their lives. Frequently it's a matter of life or death. Conditions such as diabetes and high blood pressure are often very real signs that extra weight is taking its toll on your body—both are precursors of heart disease, the number one cause of death in the United States today. And yet when you follow a safe, nutrient-rich diet and lose weight, you can reverse and/or prevent such debilitating results. And that's just what Jasper, age 26, did by beginning his Inner Compass journey with me and following it up with my eating and fitness plan. Starting out at 350 pounds, Jasper was able to get off his high blood pressure medication after just seven weeks on my eating and fitness plan. These results were so powerful for him that he truly realized we are what we eat. Suddenly it was clear how badly he had been treating his body. Given both his age and his commitment, it didn't take him long for the eating plan to make an impact and for Jasper to turn his life around. I kept telling him that if he takes small steps every day, it really pays off.

As I always remind my clients, your body wants to be healthy. And you will see in Part 2, where I describe my eating plan in full, that when you take processed foods and all the unnatural additives out of your diet, your body says, "Thank God you're hearing me now!" Your body knows good food and it will respond quickly.

Another client, Kathy, a former dancer now in her later thirties, was so overweight at 5'4" and 225 pounds that she had developed both diabetes and sleep apnea. At night in order to sleep, she had to attach a CPAP device to her face so she could breathe and not die. She had begun to feel so uncomfortable and dependent on the machine, she finally reached a breaking point and began my program. After five weeks of changing the way she eats and beginning a simple workout routine, she had lost 25 pounds and no longer needed her face mask. But what made the most impact on Kathy, even more than the weight loss, was overcoming the hurdle of not having to be hooked up to a machine at night. "I hated that machine! It was such a symbol of all that was wrong with my life. Now that I'm off it and losing weight, it feels like I can do so much more. I know I can do it!"

Witnessing these clients and so many more make huge changes not only in the way they eat and live each day but in how they think about themselves motivates me even more. These real stories are what keep me going in my work and in my life, inspiring and motivating me to continue on my path. These wonderful people can also be models for you. So ask yourself, is your health worth saving? Are you ready to make your health a priority in your life?

Turning points that motivate people to get ready depend on many variables. For some, like Taylor, it's a scary health report; for others it's more subtle or internal, such as the loss of a relationship, a job, or quality of life. Sometimes someone in their life touches a deep enough place to motivate them to make a change. Marguerite, a 38-year-old mother of two, said what finally made her feel ready to do the necessary work to lose weight and get in shape was when she learned that her kids were embarrassed to be seen with her in public. "I saw the shame on their faces, and it finally sank in. I couldn't live this way one more day. What kind of role model was I to them like this?" Marguerite was 5'6" and had reached over 300 pounds. She always had tended to be overweight, but after the births of her two children, she had put on an additional 120 pounds in an eight-year span.

A turning point that enables someone to feel ready doesn't always have to be dramatic. In other words, you don't have to be facing 100 pounds of extra weight to come to a place where you can truly say to yourself, "I am ready." What all these catalysts for change have in common is this: They force a person to take responsibility for themselves. And this is what being ready truly means.

So how do we get ourselves to take responsibility for our lives, our health, and our destiny? First, we have to get our baggage under control, get past our fear of the great unknown, and stop blaming everyone else for our problems. But if you don't stop and take in who you are—your history, your weight, your strengths and your weaknesses—then you inevitably will find yourself back where you started. It's easy to avoid this step and go right to the diet, which is so much more concrete.

It's a Question of Baggage

Whenever I talk to people about fear of the unknown, I always remind them that we all get comfortable in our worlds and don't want to change. Before you even try to put your baggage behind you, you have to look at it and see it for what it is. You might be saying to yourself, "I don't want to open that Pandora's box! It's just too scary." But you need to open up that box, as bad as those feelings or memories might be, so that you can see what it is you're afraid of. By continuing to avoid those skeletons in your closet, you only give those old bones more power.

I've found that the biggest avoiders tend to carry their emotional scars and injuries as a badge of honor. They dwell on their painful past, their disappointing relationships, their lackluster careers, and get wrapped up in the turmoil of it all. These old familiar negative feelings and situations are comforting in a weird way. But more important, they are a total distraction from taking responsibility and moving on.

If you say to yourself, "Today I am going to take one small step," you create positive momentum for change. Even if that step is simply recognizing how bad a situation is, how much it hurt you, whatever that truth is, then there is only one way to go—up!

One client, Tara, a mother of three, comes to mind. Tara is a lovely young woman, but she is used to carrying a lot of pain and sadness inside of her. She came to me looking for an answer, something to guide her in the right direction. Yes, she wanted to lose weight, but before I would even talk to her about weight loss and fitness, I sat down with her so that she could tell me about the hardships she had experienced. By simply expressing these sorrows to me, she began releasing their hold on her. With more and more honesty, she was able to gain some distance from her pain, see herself as separate from what had happened to her, and begin anew. Of course, it would be a lifetime of letting go of these feelings, but she had to start somewhere, and she did. And so can you.

Another woman with whom I worked was what I call "the classic avoider." Avery was very pretty, very funny, and very overweight. She never wanted to be truthful with herself about what she was feeling and what had happened to her. She would always say, "Everything is fine." When I would press her, she would say, "If I'm not the funny fat girl, then who am I?"

At 280 pounds, Avery was hiding behind this image of herself because she was so afraid to really look at herself. She had only small mirrors throughout her house—nothing full-length! I would say to her, "Baby, you need to look at the whole picture. Whether you like it or not, you need to look at the whole picture." It was easy to love herself from the neck up, but what was harder was the fuller reality of who she was, baggage and all. "I really like my face, but I don't want to look at the rest of my body," she'd say to me. Until we are able to look at ourselves fully in the mirror, whatever we've been through will remain heavy baggage, acting like a terrible anchor, weighing us down in unhealthy, deep waters. We need to separate ourselves from our baggage, to *see* it instead of *be* it.

Moving Beyond Fear and Blame

Sometimes clients come to me wanting and willing to take charge of their lives. They begin the Inner Compass plan, they start to eat right and exercise. They even begin to lose weight. And then after two weeks of progress, I see them backsliding. When this happens, I often return to my very first question: "Are you *really* ready to take responsibility for your life?" What I soon uncover is that despite their best intentions they get caught in one of two things: fear of moving forward, which usually stems from a fear of leaving what's familiar and a fear of what lies ahead (the unknown), or a tendency to blame others for their situation. Whether it's fear or a tendency to blame, the result is the same: an inability to take responsibility for their part in their lives. Here's what I mean.

It is perfectly natural to fear change. Who doesn't? For Mark his fear of changing the foods he eats was terrifying. He said to me, "How can I not eat my two Egg McMuffins for breakfast? Drink my four cans of Mountain Dew each day? And have a frozen pizza for dinner?"

The first thing I said to Mark was this: "Relax. I am not going to tell you to stop eating all the foods you love, even if they are filled with fat and processed crap. All I am going to do is ask you to eat less of what you love to eat and drink. Instead of three or four cans of Mountain Dew, drink one can. Instead of two Egg McMuffins, eat one. Instead of an entire frozen pizza, eat half."

Mark looked at me and said, "Really? I can still do that and lose weight?"

And my answer was yes.

Here's my reasoning: All change is difficult. So it's important that you make big changes gradually. If I had told Mark that he wasn't allowed to drink his soda or eat his fast food, I doubt he ever would have gotten past the third week of the program. By telling him to eat less, I kept the change within the realm of what was familiar. As a result, he was not only able to reduce the amount of these so-called bad foods, but he also felt more confident moving forward. As he said to me, "I never knew I could do it—but I did!" And that's what needs to happen: You need to understand what your fear is, that you can handle it, and that you can pass through it. Where is Mark now? It's three years later, and he has moved from a small town in Missouri to Seattle and opened a cleaning business that has since tripled in volume. He has also kept off the 76 pounds he lost!

Many men are similar to Mark. In my experience, men tend to get caught in their fear in a physical way, at a food level, so to speak, which is exactly why I zeroed in on his three most favorite food items. Women tend to experience their fear in a more general, emotional way. Take Karin, for example. Karin, a forty-something lawyer, was making great progress on the diet, having lost 7 pounds in the first two weeks. She was also doing well with her walking routine and had just started adding in some of the strength training (you will learn all about the diet and fitness program in Parts 2 and 3). However, she came to me to say, "I just feel so nervous all the time. I'm doing exactly what we planned, and I do feel better about my body, but I'm just afraid of going back to all my old ways that got me in this place to begin with." When I tried to help her put into words exactly what was making her nervous, Karin said, "I don't even know where to begin. I just keep thinking of my mother and how she always berated me for being overweight as a kid. The more I ate, the more she told me that no man would ever marry me. I really resent her for that. Now look at me. I am forty-two, fat, and not married. Just like my mother predicted."

Now, I am not a therapist, nor do I function as one for my clients. But what I can do is make the suggestion, based on my knowledge and experience, that weight loss and fitness have as much to do with clearing away your baggage as they do with diet or exercise. It's not so much that the physical exercise and less processed, more nutrient-dense foods wipe away your problems; rather, it's that when you begin to take care of yourself physically, you develop more stamina—physical, emotional, and mental—for managing the complexities of life, including your feelings. For me, working out has always helped me manage stress and deal with my emotions. After working out, my head is clearer and I feel more in control of things in my life. This clarity of mind keeps whatever negative feelings I am experiencing—fear of change, fear of the unknown—small, enabling me to push through to the other side and move on.

Starting with your physical body—through diet, fitness, or both—gives you confidence, the essential ingredient you need to let go of old behaviors and feelings that are no longer working for you so that you can turn to a new way of living that is all about self-empowerment.

Karin was a tough case to crack. She was still very much holding on to her past and her anger and resentment toward her mother. What I tried to help her see is that her health and her life are more important than those feelings. What was she afraid of, I asked her? Being alone? Not having her mother's attention? Or not having her mother to blame for being overweight, forty-two, and unmarried?

After a few weeks of helping her get to the point of assuming some responsibility for her overeating (after all, she finally admitted, it wasn't her mother who told her to eat), she refocused her attention on her original goal: to lose weight.

Cecily was another classic example of someone who was unwilling to take responsibility for herself. No matter what my advice, how gentle my encouragement, Cecily always felt all her problems were someone else's fault, and her biggest defense mechanism was crying. Instead of confronting anything or anyone, all she wanted to do was hide or agree and then cry about it later, saying how victimized she felt. Any kind of controversy made her retreat— whether it was a discussion at work or what to eat that night for dinner.

Crying and eating became her twin tormentors, keeping her from being able to grow into any confidence to change. She would cry at the slightest challenge. She simply couldn't deal with confrontation of any kind, an indication that she was resisting true change. Then I pointed out how her tears were merely an evasion tactic, meant to distract her (and everyone else) from the real problem. So how did I help Cecily turn it around and enable her to find the reservoir of inner strength? I got in her face and made her confront me. At first, she kept wanting to fall back on those tears, and I'd simply say to her, "You are an adult. Now talk to me and stop all that blathering. Your tears are just an escape." When she began to get in touch with her pain, she realized that retreating and eating weren't working anymore. I kept making her talk to me and encouraged her to confront all the people who let her get away with this. In time, she realized that she had begun taking care of herself and was taking responsibility for her actions. And when she started taking care of herself, the tears dried up.

Getting past your fear of the unknown and stopping your habit of blaming others for your current circumstances—whatever they are—are huge steps toward taking responsibility for yourself. Let me assure you, this is not a one-step process; rather, it's a one-day-at-a-time process. Our fears and baggage don't disappear into thin air, never to be seen again. They reappear again and again throughout our lives. I should know. I had to go through a similar process myself.

For a very long time, I have had no relationship with my own father. Of course, this absence in my life is still a source of pain, but over the years of trying to be truthful with myself and shifting into self-responsibility mode, the power of this pain to ruin or upset my life has begun to dwindle.

Sure, when certain events crop up and I am reminded of my father and his absence in my life, feelings of being unworthy surface. I have to live with that. Those feelings and memories don't disappear, and I still work on this issue all the time. But when I was younger how I dealt with these intense feelings was different and self-destructive. I would run my body into the ground in a masochistic kind of way, creating a self-sabotaging cycle that only hurt me. In a weird way, there was some comfort in what I was doing—

I would use the pain as a motivation to push myself harder. But in a sad way, I was pushing myself to extremes in anger. The more I pushed, the more stuck I was in the old hurt.

When I finally reached the point where I saw what I was doing to myself, I was able to take off the coat of pain I'd been wearing for over thirty years. I finally had the guts to say, "I can't do this anymore—who does this benefit?" Being able to be objective about the pain—and see it instead of be it—made all the difference in finding another way of dealing with my relationship with my father.

So be gentle and kind with yourself, and remind yourself that every time you resist the urge to eat out of fear or resentment or a sense of injury and consciously make a different, more positive choice to improve your health, you are taking responsibility for yourself.

The Three Rs

Once you've looked at yourself in the mirror, inside and out, and created an objective distance from your baggage, you have reached the place of really being ready. You have, in fact, jump-started your Inner Compass journey, because you have shown yourself that you are capable of change.

Whether you've been through a health scare, experienced an emotional turning point, or simply reached a place of realizing that your old habits are not working for you anymore, you have changed your position in relation to your feelings.

From this point, I suggest that my clients do what I call the three Rs— relax, respect, and reinforce—to help them solidify this first step of their Inner Compass journey. When you relax your body and mind, when you develop respect for your body, and when you begin to reinforce positive be- haviors, you truly are ready to take responsibility and change your life. Let's take a closer look at the three Rs.

Relax

In my initial session with a client, the first thing I do is say, "Relax." With this suggestion I am in fact saying two things: "Relax and take it one day at a time," and "Trust me and trust the process you are embarking on." When the fear begins to gather in the back of your throat, when you wake up in the middle of the night and find yourself pulling open the refrigerator door, just stop. Breathe in. Breathe out. Think about how you want your life to be in a different place.

When I say relax, I mean it in both attitude and behavior. As an attitude, I want you to chill, to take the edge off, to go easy on yourself. As a behavior, I really want you to calm your mind and body down!

Here are some suggestions for helping you to relax:

- Do yoga.

- Take a walk.

- Sit down on the floor in a cross-legged position and meditate; begin by focusing on your breath. This will help you bring an overall calmness to your mind and body.

- Read a book.

- Build something with your hands.

- Garden.

We all live fast-paced lives that get us very wound up. We need to stop and decide, "Do I really need to get so wrapped up in the little things of life?" One technique that I use a lot to help keep me relaxed is writing down a list of what I need to do on a daily and weekly basis. Taking the information out of my head and putting it onto a piece of paper (or into my Black-Berry) helps me find balance. If I don't write the list, I get unfocused and take on the stresses of my life. Of course, relaxing doesn't mean forgetting about what you need to do but learning how to better manage what you do need to do.

So as you go through the list above, ask yourself, "What helps me to relax?" At first, relax may seem like a purely physical word or activity. But the more you do it, finding one or two or three things you enjoy doing that help you unwind, and be more at peace within yourself, the more you will see that the greatest impact of relaxing is in your mind. A relaxed state of mind is one that helps you stay balanced in your life.

What helps you maintain balance? The answer always lies in two things: managing your time efficiently and creating "me" time each day in which to relax, so that you stay grounded and in touch with your inner self. So much of the Inner Compass work I am asking you to do is about learning how to get and stay in touch with yourself. When you are connected to this place inside yourself, you will have the confidence and energy to stay motivated and keep moving forward.

Respect

Remember how I learned that the best way I could take care of my body is by treating it as a sacred vessel, the only one I have on this planet? When you begin to think of your body as a vessel to treasure and take care of, then you actively show respect for your body, mind, and soul. Respect becomes a tangible thing, a concrete action.

No matter what ideas you have about what your body should look like, it's more about how you respect your body at the starting point. As you will soon see in the very next chapter, you have to accept yourself, warts, pounds, and all. You've got to own what you've got and then own it with all you've got. Like I always say, "If I don't love me, how is anyone else going to love me?" With acceptance comes respect.

There's always a way to criticize or judge—but what's the point? Ask yourself, "Why do I need to focus on that?" You would never nitpick your friends, so why would you do it to yourself? You need to ask yourself when it became okay to constantly berate, judge, and find fault with yourself.

Reinforce

When you renew your commitment each and every day, you reinforce your forward momentum, remind yourself of your goals, and refresh your confidence that you can and will achieve those goals.

Reinforcing your commitment is a constant, lifelong responsibility. Each day, you need to positively affirm all that you are doing for yourself. When you lay down the groundwork in the beginning, you prepare yourself for staying on track when it becomes harder. It's like any relationship, with both ups and downs. Sure, it's easy to love your partner when you are in a new relationship, but when the patina of new love fades and the first differences and challenges occur, which they inevitably do, then you need to be able to reach inside yourself and find that other layer of trust and love. The same is true of your relationship with yourself. When you reinforce your commitment to taking care of yourself, you are sending the message to your heart and mind that you are indeed your own best friend.

You're More Ready than Ever Before

In this chapter, you have heard the stories of various people and how they came to their point of reckoning, as well as my own challenge to separate myself from my baggage. I hope that you found encouragement and inspiration in these stories and the inspiration to examine your own situation.

Let me ask you a few questions and see if you now feel more ready to take charge of your life.

1. Is there any event that has happened in your life that makes you think you are ready to take charge and change your life?

2. What are your fears, if any, about making such a big commitment to change?

3. Are you ready to stop blaming others for your problems?

4. Are you ready to take responsibility for your life?

5. Can you tell yourself what your goals are?

6. Can you name three things that help you relax?

7. Do you trust the process?

8. Do you trust yourself?

9. Can you suspend disbelief and trust in a Higher Power, God, yourself, or the Universe to help you through this period of change?

10. Do you want to treat your body with respect, learn to cherish it, and make it the vessel it was always meant to be?

Answer these questions openly and honestly. Write down your thoughts. Keep your notebook, journal, or computer nearby. Use your responses as a way to continually stay in touch with what you are thinking and how you are thinking about yourself and your goals.

My plan is all about being honest with yourself, once and for all, and finally deciding that you really *do* want to make a change in your life and that you really *are* worth it. You and I both realize that it will be tough, but I can promise you that the hardest thing to do is to really learn life lessons, and there is where the change happens. I believe that your truest clarity is in the free fall of life. It is time to make that first step into a whole new world and begin a brand-new journey. You are worth it. With my help, you are going to have everything that you want, and you will reach any and every goal that you put out there. All you have to do is believe, and with that belief comes results. Aren't you tired of being in the passenger seat of your own life? It is time to jump into the driver's seat, grab the wheel, and put the pedal to the metal. It is going to be the best feeling in your life, because today is the day that you are going to put yourself at the top of your priority list and take charge of your life. Today is the day that you say, "I'm worth it and I want it all!" Today is the day that you are going to take charge . . . now!

TWO

Accept Where You Are and Forgive

— Step Two —

The next step in retraining the way you think about yourself and finding your Inner Compass is by accepting where you are right now, and that entails brave honesty. Look in the mirror. Are you overweight? Do you want to slim down? Do you want to tone and strengthen your arms and legs? Get rid of your belly roll? Touch your toes and walk to the mailbox without panting?

In the last chapter, you began the process of getting past your fear and your habit of blaming others for the problems or challenges in your life, so that you can achieve emotional distance from your baggage. This distance makes it possible for you to take that first step to take charge of your life.

Now in this chapter, you will be asked to summon the courage to *accept and forgive* exactly who is facing you in that mirror. When you can accept who you are and where you are, then you know you are dealing with yourself honestly. This is a kind of blank-slate test: By accepting who you are, you give yourself permission to change what you don't like about yourself and move on. However, when you kid yourself and pretend, for whatever reason, that you are happier, slimmer, and more in control of food than you really are, you not only create a big fat obstacle to achieving your goals, you also undermine your confidence in your ability to do so.

And right after you accept yourself, you need to forgive yourself—forgive all the false starts, failed diets, and self-sabotaging decisions you've made in the past. Then the permission to change becomes an invitation to achieve your goals.

When you take this time to reconnect with your body, you create the opportunity to stay grounded in yourself, strengthening your connection to your heart. As you will soon see, this heart-mind connection is vital to truly making the Inner Compass plan work for you

Look in the Mirror

Who is the real you? I'm going to ask you to do two things. Neither one of them is going to be easy. In fact, both tasks might make you feel uncomfortable. But remember what we learned in the previous chapter about how to create distance between you and your baggage, and about the Three Rs—relax, respect, and reinforce. When you help yourself relax, train yourself to respect your body and treat it with care, and reinforce this new way of prioritizing your time, you in turn reinforce your commitment to your goals, making them more within your reach. So here we go. You're going to need a paper and a pen. You can use a notebook, a spare piece of paper—whatever is handy.

Exercise

1. The first thing I am going to ask you to do is look at yourself in the mirror. You can take off your clothes or not. What matters here is that you take a long, hard look at the image staring back at you.

2. Now, write down what you see. Describe yourself—physically and emotionally. Write down every word that comes into your head.

3. Now read back over what you've written. Is every word you've written down true?

Remember my client Avery, who had only small mirrors in her house, nothing that showed her entire body? She's a perfect example of someone who needs to accept herself in a full way in order to move on. While I encouraged Avery to continue to love her pretty face, I wanted her to realize that all bodies look different and function differently. When people free themselves of their pain and baggage, they actually become more objective about themselves. They are paying closer attention to who and what is around them, and they can see how different we all are and that there is no perfect man or woman. Granted, it was scary for Avery to look at herself in a full-length mirror, but once she reached that place of acceptance, she paused. She needed to make this pause before she could begin to change.

Many people like to run toward the idea of change without taking this important step of self-acceptance. They get carried away in the rush to change without accepting who they are, only to find themselves back at square one in a few months. This is why so many diets work—but only in the short term. When people get in touch with what will really make them ready—uncovering who they truly are and accepting that person—then and only then are they prepared to make real, lasting changes.

As you journey away from a place of constant judgment of yourself, you will realize how much time you have been spending needlessly comparing yourself to others. Acceptance comes only without judgment.

During one season of *The Biggest Loser,* I had a young woman on my team who was very caught up in comparing herself to everyone else at the Ranch. Gaby was losing weight more slowly, and she had more trouble with the exercises. Each time she compared herself to the other women, she'd begin doubting herself again. Did I try to tell her that she should lose more, work out harder? No. I sat her down and said, "Honey, you're different from those other women. You have a thyroid problem, and the medication makes weight loss slower for you. Your body composition is different, so working out is harder. These are the cards that have been dealt to you. Either you can accept those cards or you can live your life from someone else's vantage point, not your own. Accepting and owning yourself means accepting all of you—your history, your body, and even your genetics!"

At first, Gaby got defensive and said, "But what about Isabelle? I am working out ten times harder and it's so much easier for her. Why?" I quietly said, "But Isabelle has her own cards. You can't compare yourself to her or to anyone else. This is your life, your body, and you have to deal with yourself from that deck of cards."

Before even thinking about what you want to change about yourself, you need to be able to see yourself honestly for who you are right at this minute in your life. You'll see soon that I am going to show you many tools you can utilize to make real, lasting changes—but not until you accept yourself now.

Reconnect with Your Body

One of the most important ways to truly accept who you are and where you are now is by connecting (or reconnecting) to your body. I don't just mean staying in touch with how your body feels and what signals it is sending you. I also mean staying connected to how you think and feel about your body. Over the years, having worked with many different types of people, I have observed that some of those who have the hardest time with this step of acceptance are those who stay detached from their bodies. My client Kevin is a perfect example of how important this step is. He would constantly focus on the future and promise me that he wanted to change. "I just want to get out of this body!" he'd say in almost a panic. I would tell him, "Slow down. Before you can move ahead, you have to give yourself time to connect with the body that you're in right now." People who are used to not liking their bodies tend to overlook or disregard their bodies—they pretend as if they are just heads walking around on sticks!

Gary was another example of a guy who had trouble staying inside his body long enough to make a connection. He had gained a lot of weight and then lost and gained it back again. His flesh had lost a lot of its elasticity and hung down in pockets. Gary had become so self-conscious that he didn't want to take his shirt off in front of anyone, even himself. Each day as we worked out together, we would work on the Inner Compass steps. I would acknowledge and reinforce his accomplishments and his growing confidence. Slowly, he began to see all the good I saw in him, and gradually he internalized all of it. And when he started feeling better physically too, it was as if he had created his own momentum.

It's always important to keep in mind that small milestones have the ability to grow in significance. Frequently when I work with groups, either on the show or outside of it, I will gather the group to do a review of their accomplishments. I'll ask, "Do you remember when you could barely jog for five minutes, and now you are up to fifteen? Do you remember when you couldn't lift a 5-pound weight, and now you're up to ten? Do you remember that when you arrived here you weighed 237 pounds, and now you weigh 189?"

You can do this same kind of accomplishment review on your own. As you move through this book and understand more about the Inner Compass work, its steps, and how they prepare you to maximize the eating and fitness plans (Parts 2 and 3), you will want to review your accomplishments—not just to add to your confidence but to reinforce your commitment to taking charge of your life.

Sit with yourself at least once a week and bring to mind each physical accomplishment that you have achieved in the last few days. Sometimes I refer to this time as "meditation," but you don't have to call it anything special. Just get into the new habit of letting that moment turn into more moments of focusing on yourself and allowing this "me" time to bring you to a more positive sense of yourself. The moments will soon add up, and you will gradually be rewiring that mind-heart connection, moving it from negative to positive.

Reconnecting with Your Body: An Exercise

So how do you reconnect with your body? You pay attention to it. You feed it and nourish it. You make your body move. Your body is a physical entity and will therefore respond to physical stimulation and physical care. And you fake it till you make it. This is especially true when you are dealing with obese people. There is a fine line to finding the acceptance and to finding what you love under all that fat.

One of the most powerful ways we can reconnect with our bodies is through our five senses. Here are some suggestions for getting inside your body, feeling it, and paying attention to it:

- Sit comfortably in a chair or cross-legged on a soft supportive surface. Close your eyes and take a breath.

  - Relax the muscles of your face.

  - Relax the muscles of your jaw.

  - Relax the muscles of your neck.

  - Keep breathing slowly in a relaxed manner, without effort.

  - Relax your shoulders.

  - Relax your back.

  - Relax your stomach and torso muscles.

  - Relax your hips.

  - Relax your arms and hands.

  - Relax your calves and thighs.

  - Relax your ankles and feet.

  - Breathe in and out.

  - Now do a slow body scan and see how you feel.

- Take a walk in your neighborhood or down a city street.

  - Feel the air across your face.

  - Listen to the sounds. Do you hear birds? Traffic? People talking or shouting? Cars honking?

  - How do your muscles feel? Your feet? Your arms, legs, back?

- Kick off your shoes and socks and sit comfortably in a straight-backed chair. Focus on breathing while you keep your posture upright. Keep your belly firm, so you keep oxygen flowing. Now visualize that you are in a cold room and can see your breath going in and out.

- Savasana is the final pose of any yoga practice, when you lie on your back on the floor on a mat with your palms up and your arms and legs opened naturally. This "corpse pose" rewards the body,

Some people who are having trouble with accepting their bodies are actually obsessed with their bodies. It's almost an inverse of the detachment described above. When I was working with some of my Hollywood clients, they would pay so much attention to their bodies that their ability to see what lay before them in that mirror was actually distorted. Psychiatrists call this phenomenon body dysmorphic disorder, and it is often associated with people suffering from eating disorders such as binge eating, bulimia, and anorexia. Ironically, body dysmorphia is similar to the detachment that many overweight people have—just in an inverse way. Their attachment to their bodies is so distorted that they can no longer see the person standing in the mirror's reflection. Like wearing glasses, they have become unable to see straight. I mention this situation here because I think it is relevant to how important it is to maintain a healthy connection to your body and what truly being honest really means.

acknowledging all of what you've done during that yoga class. But you can do—and deserve—this special pose anytime. The main point is sitting in that place in your mind and giving that moment to yourself. Maybe you're on the train or in the car on the highway. Try to find an oasis during the course of your day.

When you reconnect with your body, you are moving one step closer to truly being able to change from the inside out.

Forgive Yourself

Once you accept yourself, you need to forgive yourself. Forgive yourself for all the diets you've tried and failed; forgive yourself for all the bags of potato chips you've eaten; forgive yourself for all those days you watched television instead of exercising. No matter how much you have to lose or where you want to be or go after this point, you need to give yourself a pass for all the times in your past that didn't work for you. No matter how bad a situation you are in, you have a chance to change it for the good. So instead of dwelling on the past and putting on that coat of pain, hatred, and betrayal that has been keeping you warm, you can discard it. You have to forgive yourself for letting yourself get this far and give yourself permission to move ahead.

Forgiveness is letting go and turning your white knuckles back to a normal color. It takes a lot of strength and energy, but at some point you have to surrender to the ride. Remember how one of my biggest sorrows is the absence of a relationship with my father? When I hear the word *forgiveness,* I think of that issue. I go right back to when I was young, in my early twenties, questioning myself, "Why am I not good enough?" I spent a lot of time feeling the pain and internalizing the bad feelings. Then when I was thirty, I thought I was ready to forgive my father for being so out of my life. But when I sat down to write him a letter, it turned into a scathing indictment. I was still so attached to my anger and hurt that it was impossible for me to forgive him. It wasn't until about five years ago that I was really able to forgive him.

Forgiveness is not a two-way street; it doesn't have to be reciprocal, and often it is not. In order to forgive my father, I had to accept that all those years of not showing up for me, of not allowing or welcoming me into his life, were about him and not me. And what finally pushed me over this enormous hedge? I didn't want to carry the anger inside me any longer. I didn't want the burden of the pain. I knew that I may not ever hear the words "I'm sorry" uttered from his lips, but I wasn't going to wait for those words any longer. I had to move on.

And what does that feel like, moving on? It's liberating beyond words.

I have worked with all kinds of people, many of whom have shared with me horror stories of being raped, molested, and abused. They have a lot to mourn, a lot of pain to acknowledge. But they, too, have a choice: to stay inside the cloak of pain or take it off. Now, don't get me wrong. This is enormously difficult. It takes great emotional effort and willingness to be vulnerable. But it is possible. For when you are victimized once in your life, it becomes all too easy to be that victim for the rest of your life—even after the experience or the event has ended. Then it becomes your responsibility to forgive so that you can go on. You have to take an enormous leap of faith that on the other side of forgiveness lies freedom—your freedom.

Many of my clients have eased their pain with food. They have used food as medicine. When they accept who they are and where they are, and begin to forgive those who have hurt them, including themselves, they then allow self-worth to come back in and take care of them. And when they realize that playing the victim doesn't help anyone—especially themselves—they can finally sleep well at night. Forgiveness is not only the key to weight loss, it's the key to living your best life.

The Act of Forgiveness Is Difficult

And yet forgiving ourselves is difficult. We know this because of how difficult it is to forgive others who have hurt us or caused us pain. Bring to mind a grievance or act of betrayal someone committed against you. Draw both the experience and the person into your mind. Now how do you feel? Angry? Resentful? Still pained? If you feel any negatively charged emotion toward the person or feel actual pain about the experience or event itself, then it's safe to say you have not forgiven that person for hurting you.

Let's shift the focus to you now. Think about yourself and write down three things you conceive of as your failings or weaknesses. Next to each of those failings, write down an explanation for them.

For instance, when I asked my client Pam to do this exercise, this is what she wrote down:

Fat—because I eat too much

Scared—because I feel so alone

Lazy—because I have no energy

I then asked Pam if her three reasons were unchangeable or static. And she said no. I asked her to explain, and she told me, "Well, I don't have to eat too much, I do have friends, and I guess I could be more energetic." Exactly. In all three cases, Pam was able to see that her situation could be different. When I pointed this out to her, she also saw where I was heading. "So you mean I could also change the feeling that I'm fat, scared, and lazy?" The answer is yes.

What I then did with Pam was to ask her if she could find it in herself to forgive the person who thinks she is fat, the person who thinks she is scared, and the person who thinks she is lazy. That person, of course, is herself. Pam's answer to this, too, was yes.

Me Time

We all know it's important to carve out time for ourselves so that we can stay grounded and better in touch with who we are and how we feel. From this centered place, we make better decisions and are happier and more content in our lives. In this chapter, you have begun to be more honest with yourself. In the next few chapters, you are going to begin getting closer to your goals because you are going to understand what it is you want to change about the way you live now. When you begin by telling yourself the truth about what you want and where you are right now in relation to what you want, you have to do so without criticism or judgment. You need to begin to cultivate patience, for this is a process and it will take the time it takes.

One of the most useful ways to make sure that you give yourself this necessary patience is by making sure you set aside time for yourself each and every day. You will definitely need this time to do the fitness program that is outlined in Part 3 of this book. You will definitely need this self time in order to relax and become more in tune with your body and what it needs. But in the most simple way, when you set aside time to do anything for yourself, you are making a conscious choice to take care of yourself. It is this attitude, followed by the reinforcing behavior, that will act as the most positive reinforcement for your new commitment to taking charge of your life.

Exercise

1. Write down a list of five things to do that will give you pleasure, make you feel healthy, or give you comfort.

2. How long does each of these activities take? Fifteen minutes? Twenty minutes? Thirty minutes? Sixty minutes?

3. Now look at your schedule. Where can you best fit in any one of these activities during your week? Try to fit in at least two activities on at least two or three days each week.

4. Commit to this newly scheduled activity for two weeks and see how it feels.

Moving On

Accept yourself. Forgive yourself. People are so fixated on "tell me what I need to do" that they often miss the forest for the trees. Changing your life through diet and exercise is possible, but it necessitates truly being honest with who you are now. Once you face that person in the mirror and acknowledge him or her, faults and all, then you can put the past behind you and focus on the future. By accepting and forgiving yourself, you give yourself permission to move on from that old self, those old behaviors, those old crutches that have created obstacles in your path to freedom.

In the next chapter, you will continue to build on the first two steps of your Inner Compass plan by finding one thing about yourself to love. Sound simple? It is . . . but it's also a profoundly powerful way for you to take charge of your life now.

THREE

Love Yourself

— Step Three —

As you move through the Inner Compass plan, you are slowly but surely getting more in touch with who you really are. You are uncovering fears that have been obstacles in your way; you have begun to stop blaming others for your predicament and started taking responsibility for your health and your destiny. You have also begun reconnecting with your body and mind in a way that enables you to both accept who you are in an honest way and forgive yourself for all your past attempts that have let you down (or kept you from achieving lasting weight loss). But ultimately, the only way you can treat your body as the vessel it is and truly cherish yourself is if you love yourself.

When you find that one thing about yourself to love, you begin the lifelong process of knowing yourself and cherishing yourself. When this seed of self-respect is planted, you no longer have to think about taking responsibility for yourself; you automatically and instinctively take care of yourself in all ways—emotionally, physically, and spiritually.

In this chapter, you are going to crystallize the work you've been doing in the two previous steps by isolating one thing to love about yourself and letting this be the seed of confidence that grows for you, pushing you forward.

With this growing wisdom and self-assurance, you can then clearly articulate your goals and recommit to them.

Just One Thing

I'm not going to even bother to ask you what you don't like about yourself. I don't want to pay one more shred of attention to any part of you that is self-critical. And I don't want you to reinforce or fuel any negative thoughts or feelings about yourself by going down your laundry list of complaints about yourself, a list that keeps you entrenched and unable to truly take charge of your life.

Instead, I have a whole new plan for you. Anyone trying to lose weight and get in shape has to get back in touch with who they truly are—and that doesn't mean what they don't like about themselves. It's the exact opposite: It means finding one part of you that you love and admire. One client of mine, Trisha, used to complain all the time about the size of her backside: "I hate my big butt, I hate my big butt!" It was like a never-ending, self-injuring mantra. I told her, "Okay, I get it—you don't like your butt. What *do* you like about yourself?"

She replied, "Well, I like my smile." And yes, she had a big, beautiful, joyous smile. So for the first few weeks of our working together, all I did was remind her of that big, beautiful smile. Soon, not only did her butt get smaller, but her love of herself started to grow and grow.

This may sound overly simple, and in a way it is. And yet, when people focus on one simple facet of themselves they truly love, they begin the process of cherishing their entire self. They learn in a concrete, tangible way how to respect that self and take care of that wonderful vessel, their body.

Like many people with whom I have worked, you may find this step quite challenging. We can all get so married to the many ways we don't like ourselves that we can barely remember what we do like about ourselves. But let me assure you, I have seen even the most self-deprecating and self-critical people become absolutely liberated once they do lock into a positive sense of self. So let's focus on what you do like about yourself, so that you can plant this seed, preparing both your foundation and the roots to grow even stronger than before. You will learn a few more practical tools that will help you till the soil that is your self so that your plant will grow, and you will soon begin to feel newly empowered to honor this facet of your being in all that you do.

First, I want you to focus on one thing about yourself that you like, admire, or love. Is it your hair? Your eyes? Your smile, like my client Trisha? Your hands, knees, feet, or neck?

Maybe what you like or love about yourself is more intangible. Do you have a quick sense of humor? Are you good with people, often inspiring confidence and trust? Are you honest, trustworthy, and reliable? Kind and compassionate?

Or is that likable quality a skill you have? Perhaps you are a good bowler or a proficient knitter, or you can do a crossword puzzle fast and well. For now, all I want you to do is choose one quality, skill, or characteristic that you love or admire about yourself.

Exercise:

1. Name one thing about yourself you love.

2. Write that one quality down on a piece of paper.

3. Read it aloud to yourself.

4. Read it aloud as you smile and look at yourself in the mirror.

5. Close your eyes and focus on the word, the quality, and the feeling that it gives you.

YOUR MANTRA

The purpose of articulating one thing about yourself you love is so that you can simply and swiftly shift your focus from negative to positive each and every time a self-critical or self-doubting thought slips into your mind. Your one thing that you love should be your mantra for helping you stay focused on your goals and continuing to love yourself.

Once you have figured out at least one quality that you love or admire about yourself, think about this quality and revel in the joy and strength it gives you. Let this one thing be your mantra and your affirmation throughout this process and whenever you confront a self-doubting thought or feeling. Return to your mantra as a way to ground yourself and remind you who you are.

Building Confidence

Once you have a foothold in that place of self-love, it's important to continue to grow a loving relationship with yourself. Obviously none of us is perfect. And perfection is not our goal here. Our goal is to do our best at being our best. And that begins with setting realistic goals for ourselves, staying focused on those goals, and building confidence in ourselves. But the trick about confidence—having it and nurturing it—is that it doesn't grow in a vacuum. Confidence is a very concrete quality that is based on real experience. Remember the guy in high school with all the bravado, walking the halls with his chin up and his arms swatting the younger, smaller kids? At heart, we knew that the school bully was scared, not brave, and that the reason he picked on the small kids was to make himself feel bigger and better.

All of us have felt small on the inside, distracted by self-doubts and questions about our abilities. Such doubts and questions are what can keep us from growing confidence. But you can grow confidence—take the small and make it big. The key is figuring out the ways to make you shed the small and grow big. The bottom line is this: Confidence is not born, it's made.

Let's start by looking at the features of someone who is lacking in self-confidence. Someone without self-confidence tends to:

- Rely primarily on the approval of others to feel good about him- or herself

- Avoid taking risks because he or she is afraid to fail

- Expect things not to work out successfully

- Put him- or herself down

- Ignore compliments

In contrast, if you develop confidence, you tend to:

- Give yourself credit for trying your best

- Value effort rather than outcome

- Be comfortable taking risks

- Be unafraid of losing

- Realize that you cannot always win or succeed at everything you try

- Know you are not perfect

- Know your strengths and weaknesses

- Set realistic goals for yourself

As you can see from these contrasting descriptions, self-confidence is primarily made up of two things:

1. A *positive* attitude toward yourself and your abilities

2. A *realistic* view of yourself and your situation

It's rare that even the most confident people feel confident about themselves in every area of their lives. But what a confident person can do is be realistic about his or her strengths and weaknesses. She chooses activities and careers that match not just her interests but her skills and aptitudes. The confident person manages her fear by always knowing that failure is a possibility, but in so doing, she better prepares to achieve the goal she sets. Accordingly, she knows when to push herself out of her comfort zone and when to hold back because something is too risky.

Perhaps you feel confident in your academic abilities but less confident socially. Or you feel confident in your business acumen but not in your communication skills. Do a quick exercise.

1. Look at all the areas of your life: academics, business, artistic or creative pursuits, relationships with family and friends, athletics, personal appearance.

2. Make a list of your strengths in all those areas of your life. For instance, if you feel you are a loving mother or father, then put that

down. If you once opened your own business, write down that accomplishment.

3. Make a list of your weaknesses. And be honest—not cruel—about your weaknesses. If you can't carry a tune, you are probably not a natural singer. Does that mean you are not skilled in other areas? No. Keep trying and you will find something you are good at.

Many people with low confidence are not necessarily lacking in ability; it's their attitude of perfectionism that holds them back. If you focus too much on unrealistic expectations or the standards of others, especially those of parents or friends, you stray from your source of confidence—yourself. Self-confidence or its lack stems from many factors, especially what we learned from our parents. If one or both of your parents were excessively critical or demanding, chances are you have had a difficult time developing that inner strength of mind to believe in yourself.

On the other hand, parents who were overprotective or overinvolved may also have been a detriment to nurturing confidence in their kids. After all, if parents don't let their kids make mistakes, how can those kids learn that it's okay to try new things and make mistakes? And even our most well-meaning friends can undermine our confidence.

Ryan, one client with whom I worked, exemplified this difficulty of truly growing in confidence. It was very hard for him to acknowledge what he was able to achieve. I would hear him say, "I did that well, but so-and-so did it better." He could never own what his accomplishments were. After a few weeks of our working together, he began to get better at not comparing himself and his confidence started to build. You have to give yourself an opportunity to grow in confidence; it doesn't just magically happen.

Another woman really got in her own way when it came to giving herself an opportunity to grow confidence. Patty could focus only on her weaknesses, saying all the time, "I could have tried harder and worked harder." She could not let in any positive thoughts about herself. I told her, "I'm glad you're aware of your weaknesses, but now it's time to focus on your strengths." She then began articulating these strengths—to herself and out loud—as if they were her confidence-building mantra. Finding that one thing, that one mantra that pulls you back into your reality and gets you off autopilot, is key.

These are all factors to keep in mind as you begin to shift away from no-confidence thinking.

Setting Realistic Goals

Now you are really ready to set your goals. You're far enough along in your Inner Compass plan that you've earned the clarity of mind not only to articulate your goals to yourself but to establish them in a realistic way.

In my experience, many diet gurus and trainers misguide their clients by making them establish their goals too early in the process, before they've really done the work to know themselves and become more honest about their strengths, their weaknesses, and what it means to be really ready to take charge. So I've waited until now to ask you to clarify the goals you have for yourself. Perhaps you've been thinking about how much weight you want to lose from the very first page of this book. That's good. But now let's see how realistic those goals truly are, and make sure you are feeling prepared to achieve that goal.

1. How much weight do you want to lose?

2. How much weight, according to the Body Mass Index (BMI), do you need to lose for your health? (See the Resources section for information on the BMI and how best to use it. Keep in mind that, depending on your bone structure and overall body type, the BMI is not always an exact guide to determining your ideal weight.)

3. How much weight are you prepared to lose each week?

4. Are you ready to take an honest look at what you have been eating?

(See www.bmi-calculator.com to determine your BMI. Essentially, a BMI between 25 and 29.99 indicates you are overweight, and a BMI over 30 is obese.)

One way to determine how much weight you can lose is by determining your basal metabolic rate (BMR), which shows how many calories you are burning throughout the day. (Find your BMR at www.BMI-calculator.net/bmr-calculator/.) This figure will help you calculate how many calories you need to eat in order to lose or maintain your weight. In order to lose weight, you will need to create a deficit between what you are eating and using. In

Chapter Six, you will find information about your food journal and other tools to help you with these and other calculations. For now, I want you to begin focusing on the concepts behind the numbers.

Staying Positive

Any time you feel yourself questioning or doubting your ability to achieve your goal, return to your mantra to ground yourself in self-love. Remember, this mantra is the seed of your self-confidence.

Remember, too, that achieving any goal takes time and patience. If you slip one day, don't throw the baby out with the bathwater. Give yourself a break, acknowledge what happened, and then move on, returning to your diet and fitness goals with a renewed sense of enthusiasm. And remember, you can always fake it till you make it!

In the next chapter you will take a closer look at the way in which you talk to yourself. This "internal tape recorder" will reveal not only how you think about yourself but how these self-thoughts impact how you feel and what you do. If, for instance, a negative pattern of thoughts plays over and over in your head like a bad record, it will be very difficult for you to maintain a positive, optimistic frame of mind. On the other hand, if you create a new way of thinking about yourself, replacing a negative internal tape recording with a self-empowering one, then you will see amazing results in your life. With this layer of knowledge about yourself, you will once and for all learn how to replace the old, shameful thoughts and self-defeating behaviors with new, life-enhancing decisions and actions.

Questions to Ask Yourself

1. Are you ready to listen to yourself and let go of needing the approval of others to feel good about yourself?

2. Are you ready to take risks even with the knowledge that you may not succeed at first?

3. Do you believe in the possibility of success?

4. Are you ready to take all the "I shoulds" out of your internal dialogue with yourself?

5. Are you ready to stop putting yourself down?

6. Are you ready to accept the compliments of others?

FOUR

Change Your Internal Tape Recorder, Change Yourself

— Step Four —

Congratulations! You have now reached the fourth step of your Inner Compass journey. Are you still feeling relaxed? Are you trusting the process and respecting your body? Have you reconnected with your body and set aside that all-important "me time" so you can stay centered and grounded? Do you feel more accepting of yourself, more forgiving of your imperfections? Are your goals realistic and clear to you? If you responded yes to at least one of the questions, you are taking charge of your life. And if not, then know that soon it will all begin to come together—trust me.

As with any big life change, you have to be patient with yourself and give yourself plenty of room to absorb all the information. If you need to, go back over the exercises in the preceding chapters. You may find that you can answer some of the questions more easily, which means that you are now more ready than you were before. And keep in mind that this is a process;

it doesn't have a static beginning or a static end. It's all about living each moment of every day with increasing awareness.

These four steps of the Inner Compass plan are all about you becoming mentally and emotionally prepared to follow the eating and fitness plan. If you'd like, you can jump ahead to Parts 2 and 3 and read through how easy and straightforward the eating and workout plans really are. But know that neither dieting nor fitness alone will empower you to truly change the way you've been living and take charge of your life now. You must make the heart-mind connection for the diet and fitness plans to really have a lasting impact.

Which brings us here to the final step of the Inner Compass plan, when you change your internal tape recorder, that dialogue with yourself that reveals so much about how you think about yourself. You will soon learn how certain negative thought patterns may indeed be getting in the way of your life. When you gain additional objective distance from your thoughts, you actually create space to change what you do and how you act.

With this deeper self-knowledge, you also enable yourself to get to the root of your relationship with food and understand more clearly how you may be eating emotionally. Not only will you find a way to stop the cycle of emotional eating, you will also further reinforce your mind-heart connection so that you are in control of your eating once and for all. Once this connection is in place, you are free—free from the bondage of your food triggers and cravings; free to eat in a way that is healthy and satisfying and will make you lose weight; and free to fully take charge of your life.

Knowing Yourself

Your body is one thing, your brain another. When you reconnect with your body, you give yourself a concrete way to accept who you are and where you are now. And when you connect with your mind, by staying in touch with how you think and feel about yourself, you give yourself an opportunity to know yourself, accept yourself, and potentially change things about yourself that are holding you back in your life.

Do you know how you think about yourself? And how those thoughts make you feel and react? What attitudes and personal beliefs shape your outlook on life?

We often go through the day almost numb to our own experience. We get into our routines, rushing from one activity or obligation to another, barely coming up for air, and certainly not taking the time to pay attention to what our thoughts and feelings are telling us about ourselves. But both poets and scientists tell us that the more aware or conscious we are of our thoughts and feelings, the more able we are to choose to feel and think differently. This is especially important if a lot of our thoughts and feelings about ourselves are negative or self-critical. Indeed, it is becoming common knowledge (think Rhonda Byrne's *The Secret*) that holding compassionate or positive thoughts in our minds can boost the immune system, promote healing, lift depression, strengthen us physically, and even bring happiness. This implies that if we shift our thoughts from the negative to the positive, we can shift our behaviors and feelings as well and create our own experience.

These self-thoughts feed our emotions. We don't react to certain situations or interactions with people in a vacuum. Instead, we do so based on how we think about ourselves. That's why the more we can listen to our thoughts and hear how we think about ourselves, the more we can change negative or self-critical thoughts into positive, self-affirming feelings about ourselves. Remember finding that one thing to love? Building your confidence in your abilities? All that is grounding you. Now begin to listen to how you think about yourself. As you go through your day, pay attention to any self-thoughts. Are they negative? Positive? Encouraging?

Many of us get caught in a cycle of self-berating or critical thoughts about ourselves that wear away our self-esteem. The more conscious we become of these thoughts, the more we can choose not to believe them.

A good example of how to channel the power of one's thoughts is Kelly, a very funny stand-up comedienne I worked with a few years ago. She was great at following my eating and fitness plan, but no matter how well she was doing, how much weight was coming off, and how she was changing physically, she still felt like the fat girl inside. She hadn't done enough of the Inner Compass work to let go of what was in her way, and was stuck because she still perceived herself as the funny fat girl.

She would say, "I'm the new Kelly," and I would reply, "You're not a new Kelly. You are an improved Kelly, still attached to you." This was a big eye-opener for her. As a comedienne, she is used to being self-deprecating, so seeing all of herself, accepting and forgiving all of herself, was a hard act to change.

It all relates back to acceptance. You must accept not just who you are at the beginning of your Inner Compass journey but who you were before and who you are going to be in the future. You are all of those selves. You bring yourself with you. And in order to wrestle this tiger to the ground once and for all, you need to stop your negative thoughts from assaulting your sense of self.

Our thoughts are a window into how we conceive of ourselves—our strengths and weaknesses, our limitations and aspirations. And yet most of the time we float from one activity to the next without considering that we can choose to think in a more positive way.

As you begin to make this shift into awareness, you will find that you can also have a direct impact on how you react to certain situations and even how you feel. Our thoughts create our feelings. And when you are trying to get to the root of your relationship with food, these thoughts often trigger emotional eating.

Exercise: Time Capsule

One of the first things I do with new clients is ask them to fill out a questionnaire about how they think of themselves. Once they respond to these questions, I then instruct them to put the answers away for twelve weeks. Then at the end of the twelve weeks, I ask them to revisit the questionnaire and read through it. Why don't you try this exercise?

Here is the questionnaire:

1. What are three words that you would use to describe yourself?

2. How would your best friend describe you?

3. Tell me what you *don't* like about yourself.

4. Tell me what you *do* like about yourself.

5. What do you want to change?

6. What are your physical goals?

7. Imagine reaching your goals; what do you think that will that feel like?

8. Do you really want to make a change?

9. Why?

10. Give me an idea of your eating habits (favorite foods and trigger times—those times of the day when you are most likely to eat or snack).

11. What kind of physical activity do you do?

12. What diets have you followed?

13. What worked?

14. What didn't work?

15. Are you ready to take charge of your life?

I think you will find it enormously gratifying and reinforcing to discover exactly what you've accomplished!

Emotional Eating

Lately there has been a lot of talk about emotional eating and the reasons behind why many of us turn to food to make ourselves feel better. In other words, at one time or another we all eat even when we are not physically hungry. When we eat for reasons other than hunger, it is usually an indication that we are eating emotionally; that is, instead of feeling our feelings, we eat our feelings. As soon as a difficult emotion is triggered—fear, pain, anger, sadness, loneliness—we reach for food to push away or get relief from the feeling.

I do this just like anyone else. When I have a particularly busy schedule or I'm in the midst of taping the show, working seven days a week, I reach for food to soothe myself, to relieve the stress. But it wasn't until I was working closely with Kimberly, who was a lawyer, that my own emotional eating became clear to me.

Kimberly was very type A (like me), very disciplined (like me) and very hardworking (like me). For weeks I watched as she changed her eating habits and worked out more and more, but I knew something was up because she wasn't losing the weight she should have been, given her diet and exercise.

One day, we were doing a simple exercise in our Inner Compass work and she let it slip that when she gets home at night, especially after a grueling day at her law firm, she "rewards" herself with a pizza. She explained to me, "I am so good all day. I think I just deserve to eat badly sometimes."

Hmmm, I thought to myself. There were actually two things she was doing that were preventing her from losing weight. The first was that she was eating a hell of a lot of calories in that pizza, more than she would need to feel full and satisfied. Second, and probably more important, she was eating her feelings instead of feeling them. She felt exhausted from having taken care of other people all day long and believed she "deserved" the pizza. But who was she really taking care of? Herself? Until she stopped and asked, "How do I feel? Do I really want to eat pizza and treat my body so badly?" she would continue to short-circuit her emotions, moving from her bad feelings to food without thinking.

I related to Kimberly in so many ways. When my work is so intense and I'm up at 5:00 A.M., taking care of so many people throughout the course of the day, I can get into a pattern in which I find myself saying, "I deserve to eat and drink whatever I want—that chocolate cake, for instance." But when I pay attention to how stressed and out of balance I am feeling, I stop instead of automatically turning to food.

When I realized this, a lightbulb went off: My emotional eating is the exact same thing that my overweight clients tell me about. It wasn't as if I was making super-bad food choices all the time, but I could relate to the urge. I was giving my body what my mind wanted, not what my body wanted.

I sometimes still eat emotionally—I'm not perfect. But I can maneuver around these lapses. For many, however, eating one pizza can turn into ten, and in no time you've lost your resolve, your connection to your body, and your clear view of your goals.

This happens a lot to people around the holidays. I will hear people say, "Okay, Christmas is coming and I am going to gain 5 or 10 pounds and then lose it." Then it's 20 or 25 pounds and it's spring. It's a slippery slope if you don't know your relationship with food and how your body changes. Eating bad food makes you feel bad. It literally takes away your energy, your confidence, and your motivation.

Why food? Food offers a tactile, enjoyable way to soothe ourselves. Some of us were raised by mothers who gave us a bottle or food as a way to calm or quiet us. Others may recall big dinners where family and friends gathered to celebrate their love for one another. In both situations, food is a form of love. And of course, food is meant to be enjoyed and celebrated! But what can become problematic is when we short-circuit our brain-to-body connection so that in times of stress or unease, we go to food for relief instead of processing our feelings.

Don't worry, we are not about to process all your feelings. But we are going to take a closer look at how you might be using food emotionally so that we can stop you from perpetuating the bad behaviors that follow the negative feelings.

Consider these two scenarios and see if they are at all familiar: Sally returns home after a stressful day at work to find the kitchen a mess, her two- and four-year-old kids whining after a long day at the babysitter's, and a message from her partner saying that he is not going to be home for dinner. Suddenly, all she wants to do is order a couple of large pizzas, sit down with the kids, and eat. The kids will eat a couple of slices between them and she'd have the rest of the two pies for herself.

Or try this one: Tom is at home on a Saturday afternoon by himself. He has no plans for the weekend, so he flips on the TV and decides to take a look through the freezer. And lo and behold, he finds a full carton of cookies and cream. Without a second thought, he sits himself in front of his television and polishes off the entire carton of ice cream.

How do you think Sally was feeling just before she ordered the two pizzas? And what about Tom when he flipped on the television and headed toward the freezer? There are many reasons aside from hunger that prompt people to eat—boredom, sadness, nervousness, anxiety, stress, even happiness. But if you look at what these things all have in common, it's that they are emotions, not signals of your body's need for nourishment.

When we are hungry and need to eat, our brains are hardwired to signal us that we should look for food. Yet many people also feel an urge to eat certain foods when they experience certain emotions, or when they find themselves in certain settings. And often the foods people tend to choose are those fatty or sweet foods that not only contain a lot of calories but also create food hangovers or cravings. Take our example of Sally. She was probably

ingly enough, I had been frequenting the Kabbalah Centre, having been drawn to its inclusive, welcoming sensibility and its focus on empowering people to become their best possible selves.

As a devout Kabbalist, Madonna wanted to help Rav Berg and his wife get in better physical shape. "I need you to be their cheerleader, Bob," she explained to me.

I began working closely with Rav Berg and his wife. In the process, I took my understanding of the Kabbalah to another level. In fact, the more I absorbed, the more it impacted every dimension of my life, including how I worked one-on-one with people, training them in diet and fitness.

Many people assume that the Kabbalah is simply a form of Jewish mysticism or a religious dictum. But the Kabbalah is actually one of the world's oldest forms of spiritual wisdom, offering a very modern and effective way to gain a sense of power in one's life. Similar to the Law of Attraction described in the popular book *The Secret,* the Kabbalah shows how to navigate your feelings in order to gain more positive control over your life. For thousands of years, the great kabbalistic sages have taught that every human being is born with the potential for greatness and the Kabbalah is the means for activating that potential. Specifically, I've adapted what Rav Berg teaches as the Proactive Formula to use with my clients when helping them break a cycle of emotional eating.

This is how it works. Whenever you are faced with an intense emotion, an urge to eat, or both:

1. Stop. As you did when you became aware of your negative thoughts, become aware of how you feel and what you think you want to do (eat).

2. Don't react. Just sit with your feelings or desires.

3. Let the light in and make that connection to God, your Higher Power, the Universe, or your community of love. You can even connect to that part of yourself you call your soul. This is critical, as it helps you open yourself to both the possibility and probability of change.

When you stop and become more aware of what you are doing and desiring, you take that first step to initiate change. Instead of bouncing like a pinball, you stop and become aware. Adapting this formula for using your

In the next chapter you will find many ways to help you stick to the diet and fitness plan and avoid your triggers for cravings and overeating. But in advance of that, keep these handy tips in mind:

- Get moving. Exercise helps in two ways—it boosts your mood and your resolve.

- Indulge your craving, but only in moderation. Instead of suffering through the craving or eating a bunch of different healthy snacks that just don't do the trick, treat yourself—but savor a small portion rather than pigging out. It's not realistic to think that we are going to resist our cravings all the time, but do so in small portions and use moderation.

- Wait it out. Sometimes cravings pass. Hunger won't. So if you're tempted, wait twenty minutes and see if you're still in the mood to indulge.

mind to stop negative or self-sabotaging behavior for fitness was a huge step for me, because it was immediately clear that if all the people I worked with just stopped and stayed in that one moment, they would stop mindlessly rolling into one minute and then the next minute.

In our culture, we tend to live so unconsciously; this short, simple word—*stop*—has the power to bring awareness in an instant.

Remember, this is not a diet—it's an eating plan for the rest of your life!

Weeding Your Garden

Your weeds are all the negative thoughts, words, and phrases that are constantly playing in your head and that reinforce bad behaviors, such as overeating or binge eating. Now that you've planted the good seed and begun to nurture this new growth, you're ready to start taking a weed whacker to all those weeds in your garden.

Let's take a look at all the situations in your life that create stress. When we know what situations tend to trigger us to eat emotionally and set off the

When we listen to ourselves and gain an objective distance from our thoughts, we gain the power to change those thoughts. Do this exercise.

Fill in the blanks.

1. Food is _____.

2. Food is _____.

3. Food is _____.

4. Describe what happened the last time you overate or ate a food that made you feel bad about yourself.

5. Can you describe the feeling you were experiencing at that time?

When you have to think about what food means to you—how it feels when you indulge and give in to temptation—nine times out of ten you feel bad and have negative thoughts. This is when you dialogue with yourself: *Why do I want this? How will it make me feel?* You might still do it, but you will have more awareness of your actions. Then at some point in a future dialogue with yourself, you will choose differently. You are in the process of rewiring your brain. As you will see when you integrate your food journal into your life, you will read back and remind yourself how you handled a similar situation the last time, which is why your food journal is such useful tool.

---

internal tape recorder, then we can be better prepared to make other, more self-empowering decisions. Try this exercise.

1. Make a list of all the situations in your life that cause or caused you stress. These situations or events can be either mundane or dramatic, from the death of a parent to a child's graduation, from a job change to an upcoming haircut.

2. How do you tend to react to stress? Describe all the ways in which you behave, including overeating or eating unhealthy foods, to offset or manage the stress.

3. Looking at both lists, can you imagine changing any of the ways you react or behave?

4. Now make a list of ten ways in which you can manage stress differently. Here are some examples:

- Take a walk.

- Call a friend.

- Write in your journal.

- Visualize yourself outside of the stress.

- Read a book.

- Revisit your goals and renew your commitment.

- Listen to music.

- Meditate or do yoga.

The more you can hear the negative, self-critical, or doubting thoughts when they occur, the more able you become to stop yourself from reaching for food and making a poor food choice.

———————

Congratulations—you have seen your Inner Compass through its four steps. I hope that you have gained knowledge and understanding of what may have been in your way. Remember, this is not a linear path; often it's circular in nature, asking us to return again and again to old issues, tired baggage, and old behaviors before we finally gain enough of that distance and enough of that acceptance and forgiveness to free ourselves. But keep the faith and fake it till you make it.

Onward to the eating plan of your dreams!

PART 2

Stepping Up to the Plate

When they learn the more able you become to stop yourself while reaching for treats and making a food choice.

People often arrive at my doorstep so medicated with food, they don't know or can't remember how to feel good without it. Food has been their enemy, their lover, their partner in crime. By taking the initial steps of your Inner Compass plan, you have begun to tear down the house of shame that held this negative relationship with food and started rebuilding the foundation of what is going to be your ticket to freedom, weight loss, and lasting health and well-being.

When you find your Inner Compass, you become your own best friend. I always reassure everyone willing to take this journey with me that they will soon begin to feel much better. They just need to give this new approach to managing their feelings and establishing their goals a chance to take root. Not only do you feel your mind start to shift, you also enable yourself to be open to a much healthier way of eating, which is what Part 2 is all about.

You will soon be learning a simple but tasty way of eating that is completely satisfying. You will learn how these nutrient-dense foods shower your body with what it needs and not what it doesn't. You will begin to lose weight, think more clearly, and feel so much better—about yourself, the world around you, and all that lies before you.

And the pounds will begin to come off. You start with a small snowflake, and the snowball starts to grow until it's a thunderous avalanche with a life of its own.

My eating plan has a few guidelines to get you comfortable and at ease with how to eat in a healthy way. In the beginning, you will pay attention to your food intake with some very general calorie watching, label reading, and—most important—keeping track of how you feel. I have assembled a list of foods to choose from, a great selection of quick meals, and a guide to writing all of this down in your food journal. One of the keys to this plan is making sure to eat every four hours. This not only offsets hunger but also prevents you from overeating or unnecessary snacking. Of course, I've worked in lots of tips for eating on the run and in restaurants, how to navigate travel, and what to do for parties and other social occasions when temptations to make poor food choices arise. Fueled by a lot of encouragement, as well as many anecdotes from my work with clients, you will soon have the tools and motivation to seamlessly integrate this eating plan into your life.

FIVE

It's an Eating Plan, Not a Diet

This is not a diet you go on and off. It's not a plan or program that you stick to for eight, ten, or twelve weeks, lose weight, and then stop doing. No—my eating plan is a way of forevermore changing the way you eat so that you can lose the weight you want. And once you reach that desired goal, you will be able to maintain that healthy weight by continuing to eat in the same way. This is a lifestyle, not a diet.

Again, you will be eating clean, nutrient-dense, whole foods that are high in fiber. You will be eating a healthy amount of foods from all the food groups—carbohydrates, proteins, and even fats—and you will learn about "good" foods versus "bad" foods in all these categories. I am a longtime foodie and would never sacrifice taste for bland but healthy food! And that's what I can promise you: This is not a deprivation diet, nor is it bland, boring, and without texture. You are going enjoy lots of tasty, satisfying foods that make you feel satisfied as you lose weight.

In the beginning I am going to ask you to do general calorie counting and pay attention to your portion sizes. This attention to detail is necessary in the beginning, but as soon as you get into a rhythm and know how to use both my food list and your food journal, you will be able to eyeball your foods and make good food decisions without so much time and planning. Remember, information is power, and you need this information about what you are putting into your body.

The Basics

Most of us were taught that a healthy diet is made up of three meals a day, with each meal containing a protein, starch, and vegetable. If we hadn't started processing and packaging our foods, putting it in cans and microwavable containers and building fast-food restaurants on every corner, this basic nutritional advice might have worked for us. Instead, we are a nation of overweight and obese people who are addicted to fatty, salty, processed foods that contain very little nutrition and lots of calories.

One thing I have learned and witnessed again and again with all my clients, including *The Biggest Loser* participants, is that in order to really change the way you eat and make healthy eating choices that guarantee both that you lose weight and that you keep it off, you have to learn more about the nature of food. Now, bear with me; I know you just want me to tell you, "Eat this, don't eat that, and then you will lose weight." But if I just gave you instructions like a drill sergeant in the army, you would never truly get to the point where you trust yourself to make the best food choices for you. In order to make this leap, you have to become familiar with some basic food concepts; that's where your trust in yourself begins. Again, I promise, it will not take you long to become very familiar with the basics of nutrition—maybe a week or two—but once you really absorb and internalize the information, you will never look at food the same way again. You will also have the power and the confidence to lead a life that is all about taking care of you.

The Food Groups Redefined

In order for our brains and bodies to function, we need to eat foods from the three main food groups—carbohydrates, proteins, and fats. It's key to eat the right balance of these foods:

- Protein that is low in fat—lean meat, poultry, seafood, and soy.

- Complex carbohydrates high in fiber—whole grains, vegetables, and fruit. These foods are especially rich in antioxidants, which support your immune system.

- Simple carbohydrates—high in starch and/or sugar and low in fiber—refined breads, pastas, rice, and sweets.

- Dairy—products that are lowfat or nonfat—milk, cheese, and yogurt.

- Fats that contain no trans fat, are low in saturated fat, and high in omega-3 fatty acids—olive oil, canola oil, fish oil, nuts, and seeds.

In general, you want your meals to contain a balance of 30 percent protein, 30 percent fat, and 40 percent carbohydrates (again, these carbs need to be high in fiber). Fiber is a nondigestible substance natural to fruits, vegetables, and whole grains that not only slows down the absorption rate of food but also fills you up. I like to think of fiber as the magical nutrient that allows us to eat as many fruits and vegetables as we like! It also cleanses the body of toxins, keeps our metabolism working properly, and moves the food through our system with ease. Fiber is a key ingredient to healthy eating and lasting weight loss.

As you get familiar with my food list, you will also begin to think in terms of these food group categories. This will help you think more clearly about your food choices and simplify your decisions about what to eat. Things get less straightforward and more murky, however, when you turn to processed or packaged foods.

The biggest reason behind the national obesity and diabetes crises is our overconsumption of processed foods. These foods have added ingredients that literally change their nature. In order to increase their shelf life and add flavor, processed foods are stuffed full of additives, trans fats, large amounts of sodium, and other harmful ingredients. The bottom line? Our bodies are not meant to metabolize or use the ingredients put into foods that keep them "fresh" on the grocery store shelf, in the freezer, or in the cupboard. As much as you possibly can, try to eat foods that are fresh. And if you have to eat at a fast food chain or from a package, then try to do so as infrequently as possible.

As you will soon see, my food list is simple, but it's also varied. You are going to find many foods that appeal to your taste buds and your stomach. I repeat: You are not going to be hungry on my eating plan! You will, I predict, begin to taste the real nature of foods again, and enjoy fresher, whole foods with more gusto and appreciation.

Portion Sizes

When it comes to how much of each food you should be eating, I want you to think of an empty plate. Preferably choose a 9- or 10-inch plate, not the new 11-inch style that is so in fashion now. You will fill the plate like this:

- 2 pieces of grilled chicken breast each the size of your palm (if you like to go by weight, this portion should weigh about 6 ounces cooked or 8 ounces raw)

- 2–3 fist-size portions of steamed broccoli (2–3 cups)

- 1 fist-sized portion of brown rice (1 cup)

My guidelines for portion sizes are basic, and once you get familiar and comfortable with these general serving sizes and stick to the foods on my food list, then you don't really have to worry about calories—you will automatically stay within the range for weight loss and/or maintenance. Most people find it easier to think of their foods in portion sizes, but the only foods that you really need to limit are protein and fats and those carbohydrates that are not high in fiber. There is no limit to how much fruit and vegetables you can eat! But you decide how you want to handle this. Some people like the guidelines; others prefer to restrict just the protein and fat and starchy carbs, eating as much of the vegetables and fruits as they like.

Supplements

I recommend that both women and men take three main supplements that help with their weight loss, ensure they get sufficient vitamins and minerals for optimal metabolism, boost their immune system, and protect them from degenerative diseases (such as heart disease, diabetes, and osteoporosis).

These supplements are

- Multivitamin with folic acid

- Omega-3 (EPA and DHA supplement)—fish oil or ground flaxseed

If any of these supplements come in gender-specific brands or combinations, then choose accordingly.

Eating for Weight Loss

Again, you will absolutely lose weight when you begin to follow my eating plan, but deciding how much weight you want to lose is, of course, entirely up to you.

It is absolutely crucial that you eat every four hours, which means you will probably be eating five times a day. Some people like to think of eating three meals and two snacks. What works best for me is simply keeping track of the time, looking at my watch, and saying to myself, "It's time to eat. Now what am I in the mood for?"

If you don't eat frequently, you will get hungry, and when you are trying to lose weight, getting too hungry may trigger old behaviors and bad food decisions. When you eat frequently and are eating healthy foods, you actually increase your metabolism, making it burn more calories, while at the same time you feel more balanced. Often those dips in energy or mood that we feel at certain points of the day are caused by drops in blood sugar. When you eat frequently, you avoid these dips, stay away from feeling moody, and prevent yourself from making impulsive food decisions. Many of us who are carb or sugar "addicts" actually suffer from a difficulty balancing our blood sugar. The cravings for sugar or carbs are a quick fix for the body that results only in more cravings. If you avoid these trigger foods and instead eat the foods rich in fiber, then you never get to that place of craving, and slowly but surely you will lose your sensitivity to these highs and lows of energy.

Food Group	Foods	Portion Size	Calories per Serving
Protein	Lean meat, poultry, seafood	2 palm-size pieces or 6 ounces cooked	110
Complex carbs	Whole grains, fruits, vegetables	2 fist-sized amounts or 2 cups cooked	50–60
Simple carbs and sugars	White breads, cereals, sweets	1 fist-size amount or 1 cup	80–90
Dairy	Low-fat milk, cheese, yogurt	1 fist-size amount or 1 cup	90–100
Fat	Olive oil, canola oil, nuts	1 teaspoon	45

Calories for Weight Loss

Although I don't rely solely on calories to direct my clients, I do find that especially in the beginning—for the first month or so—most women and men benefit from monitoring their calories as a way to understand how much they are eating and plan out their meals. By keeping track of their calories, they also feel more grounded and in control. (You will be asked to record your calorie intake in your food journal; see page 80.) So for those of you who are already comfortable and familiar with calorie-counting, here are a few hard and fast rules:

- You need to eat at least 1,200 calories per day, otherwise your body will go into starvation mode.

- Most people will lose weight very quickly eating between 1,500 and 1,800 calories per day.

- Many people will lose weight gradually eating between 1,800 and 2,000 calories per day.

- Once you've lost the weight you desire, you can maintain your new weight by eating between 2,000 and 2,500 calories per day if you continue to exercise regularly.

- Exercise in general burns calories, enabling you to either eat more calories or lose more weight.

Staying Within Your Calorie Goal

Most people like to eat three meals that contain about 500 calories each, with a snack of about 300 calories, which would keep you in the range of 1,800 calories per day. Again, I want you to be eating every four hours, and I don't recommend skipping meals. However, some days may not work out as planned—you get caught in traffic, you're traveling, you have to work late—whatever. Life can get in the way of even our best intentions. So if you do skip a meal, you can still fall back on your calorie counting and eat more during one meal.

You need to get in the habit of reading labels of any food that is in a package. Not only does the label list the calorie count, but it also reveals what additives might be included.

What you don't want to see on a food label:

- Fat more than 10 grams per serving

- Sodium higher than 500 milligrams per serving

- Trans fats in any amount

- Carbs more than 25 grams per serving

CALORIES PER GRAM

1 gram of carbohydrate = 4 calories	1 gram of fat = 9 calories
1 gram of protein = 4 calories	1 gram of alcohol = 7 calories

Every 3,500 calories is equal to 1 pound. So if you cut back by 500 calories per day, you should lose 1 pound each week. If you cut back 250 calories per day and increase your exercise to burn an extra 250 calories per day, you can also lose 1 pound per week.

What you do want to see on a food label:

- Total fat less than 10 grams per serving

- Sodium less than 500 milligrams per serving

- No trans fats

- Fiber in any amount

The next chapter discusses your food journal. This is the place where you will write down everything that you eat and when you eat it. This way, you keep track of the types and amounts of foods you eat, including your calories, and make sure that you are eating every four hours. As you will see, you will also be asked to write down how you feel when you eat certain foods. Keeping a record of your foods may seem like an arduous task, but it is key to becoming aware of how you eat and how it makes you feel. This is the secret to lasting weight loss and never having to diet again!

Popular Triggers to Avoid

You also want to stay away from these popular trigger foods; they not only have the power to trigger a craving but also add unnecessary calories.

- Keep your sugar substitutes, such as Sweet'n Low and Splenda, to a minimum. These are great products for adding sweetness to a beverage or cereal. But too much might trigger your craving for something really sweet—like a slice of pie or ice cream!

- Avoid foods high in sodium, including Chinese takeout, chips, canned soups, and some frozen dinners. Sodium not only makes you retain fluids but also acts as an appetite stimulant and contributes to heart disease.

- Avoid foods high in fat, including ice cream, baked goods, and chips. Some of these foods may contain trans fat, but even if they don't, the fat means you're taking in too many calories, and this will no doubt upset your caloric goals for the day.

- Avoid alcohol. An occasional glass of wine or light beer is a pleasure I don't want to deny you. But it's easy to forget that alcohol contains a lot of hidden calories—80–90 calories per glass of wine and 120 calories per beer. If you have between three and five drinks per week, that's around 250–500 extra calories per week! Alcohol also lowers our inhibitions and may lead to less-than-good food choices.

- Caffeine is a stimulant and one many of us rely on to wake us up in the morning or give us that extra oomph when our energy flags in the afternoon. But do keep in mind that too much caffeine can be bad for us, stressing our bodies, depleting our bones of calcium, and eventually making us more tired than wakeful.

Drinks

Water, water, and more water! Water keeps everything moving through you. It also enriches your skin and will help you lose weight. Drink as much water throughout the day as you can.

My food list contains other tasty drinks that are both good for you and enjoyable. And again, you want to watch any drink that contains added calories—read your labels!

What You've Been Eating: An Exercise

On day one of working with a new client, one of the first things I ask them to do is write down a list of what they usually eat. Then I ask them to write down exactly what they ate for breakfast, lunch, dinner, and snacks on the day before.

Let me share with you a couple of samples given to me by two of my clients:

John, June 20, 2007

Breakfast: no food, 1 large Coke from Dunkin Donuts (390 calories)

Lunch: cheeseburger from Wendy's (470 calories), french fries (530), large Coke (293)

Snack: bag of M&Ms (1,023 calories), large Coke (293)

Dinner: Chicken parmigiana (410 calories) with side of spaghetti (200) and red sauce (143), three beers (360)

Snack/dessert: pint of ice cream (670)

Total calories: 4,782

At 5'11", John weighs 297 pounds and wants to lose about 40 pounds. He is eating almost 2,000 more calories a day than his body needs.

Susan, May 31, 2007

Breakfast: Egg and Sausage McMuffin from McDonald's (450 calories)

Snack: Toasted bagel (310) with cream cheese (190)

Lunch: Caesar salad with chicken (190), Caesar dressing (120), Diet Coke (1)

Snack: Quaker Oats Vanilla Crunch Bar (210), mochaccino (375)

Dinner: Perdue fajita chicken breast strips (200 calories), 3 flour tortillas (300), guacamole (54), side of Uncle Ben's Fiesta Rice (200 calories), salsa (36)

Drink: two glasses of wine (160 calories)

Total calories: 2,796

Susan is 5'4" tall and weighs 200 pounds; if she wants to lose weight at the rate of 1 pound per week and her goal is to lose 50 pounds, then she needs to cut her calories down to about 1,800.

In both cases, John and Susan were eating too many calories. Most of these calories came in the form of sugary drinks and fatty snacks. This is true for many of us; with Dunkin Donuts and Starbucks on every corner, it's very difficult to turn down the temptation. Most of us don't realize how many calories we are unknowingly eating in the course of a day. Sodas at the gas station, M&Ms off someone's desk at the office, that quick snack right before dinner because you're "starving"—these all add up, and eventually they show up on your body.

The more you replace these unhealthy snacks with more nutritious and less caloric options from my food list, the less you will be drawn to these poor choices. The cleaner your food becomes, the cleaner your body will feel. You literally will begin to feel the negative backlash after eating too much sugar, salt, or fat. Your body will feel sluggish, and you will feel tired. Trust me on this—I've witnessed this reaction again and again. Of course there is some room for your favorite splurges, whether that be a small bowl of ice cream or your favorite coffee drink, but you need to strive for moderation. It's a better way of managing all the temptations in your everyday life. As you will see in Part 2, when you begin to keep a record of what you eat and drink on a daily basis, you can control such splurges with simple calorie counting.

Once you get familiar with these basics, you will be able to trust yourself to make good decisions throughout your day. I don't want you to get lost in calorie counting, measuring, and complicated recipes. Instead, you can easily refer to my food list, mixing and matching from the selection of protein, carbs, vegetables, fruits, and drinks to create simple but delicious snacks and meals. In essence, I try to put my clients on a schedule and encourage them to eat a wide variety of foods every four hours. Once you start eating in this way, you will understand why the frequency is crucial to feeling balanced. I take into account that eating in the real world involves time and money, and my suggestions won't cost you a fortune or keep you in the kitchen for hours. So even if you're a single parent or married to your career, you will find inexpensive foods that you can eat without breaking the bank or your routine.

Now, let's take a look at my food list.

My Food List

My food list is massive. Some of my clients have even called it "crazy." Why is it so long? Because I want you to be able to think about all the foods you *can* eat instead of wondering what you *can't* eat. Remember, this is a way of life, not a diet. There's room for delicious meals, decadent indulgences, and cures for your cravings. Would you be surprised to know that Häagen-Dazs ice cream is on the list? If one afternoon all you want is some ice cream, then I say go to your fridge, find that one-ounce serving of Häagen-Dazs, and enjoy it! You will know where you can cut calories in the next day or so or how much time to add to your workout in order to burn off the ice cream calories. It's much more realistic to expect that sometimes we are going to indulge our cravings rather than deny ourselves these treats for the rest of our lives. And if you have a single-serving container in your freezer instead of an entire pint or half gallon, you have built-in portion control.

When you follow my diet and fitness plan, you will not have to take a lot of time worrying about what to eat, shopping, planning, or preparing meals. My food list is meant to be your shopping guide, your meal planner, and your go-to source for all things food-related. You simply carry it with you—folded in your purse or wallet—and use it as a quick source of meal ideas. Once you get familiar with its contents (and I promise that is going to happen sooner than you think), you will simply be eating in this new, clean, and nutritious way without any forethought at all!

For Beth, the food list has been a "godsend. I just keep it with me at all times, so even when I'm feeling a bit overwhelmed and like I might do or eat something stupid, I read the list. It's that therapeutic for me." John says this about the food list: "I used to hate to shop. I live by myself and going to the grocery store felt like a waste of time, so I would always eat out. But ever since I started using the food list, I enjoy going to the store. I think it's because there is so much variety and because I know I can prepare a lot of what's on the list—it's easy."

The food list is meant to be easy. It's also meant to encourage you to try new foods and stretch your comfort zone when you are ready. It's all up to you. Though I've recommended brands of certain foods that I favor, you can find other brands that are low in fat, sodium, and additives. But make sure you check the labels carefully.

Protein

Wild salmon

Tuna

Halibut

Swordfish

Tilapia

Red snapper

Cod

Sea bass

Tuna

Lobster

Canned tuna in water (solid white or chunk light)

Extra-lean ground beef

Fillet of beef

Top sirloin

Turkey breast

Lean ground turkey breast

Skinless chicken breast

Lean ground chicken breast

Low-sodium deli slices (chicken, turkey, roast beef, boiled ham)

Turkey bacon

Canadian bacon

Eggology egg whites

Whole eggs

Protein powder (whey protein isolate) (chocolate, vanilla)

Myoplex Carb Sense protein drinks (chocolate, vanilla, strawberry)

Low-fat/nonfat milk

Low-fat/nonfat cottage cheese

Low-fat/nonfat cheese (cheddar, mozzarella, pepper jack, ricotta)

Laughing Cow Low-Fat Cheese Triangles

Raw or dry-roasted nuts (almonds, walnuts, cashews, pistachios)

Tofu

Soybeans (edamame)

All-natural peanut butter

All-natural almond butter

Fage 2% Greek-style yogurt (my new favorite obsession!)

Carbohydrates

Whole-wheat bread

Whole-wheat English muffins

La Tortilla Factory low-carb, low-fat tortillas

Wasa crackers (light rye, Crisp'n Light, multigrain)

Whole-wheat pasta

Brown rice

Brown rice pasta

Wild rice

Beans (dry or low-sodium canned) (black, white, pinto, kidney, black-eyed peas)

Lentils

Quinoa (another new obsession— quinoa is a complete protein and tastes delicious)

Lima beans

Shredded wheat cereal

Weetabix cereal

Kashi Go Lean cereal

Quaker oatmeal (unsweetened, Weight Control, Old-Fashioned)

Orville Redenbacher's plain popcorn

Vegetables (the sky is the limit!!!)

Spinach

Broccoli

Kale

Collard greens

Spaghetti squash

Green beans

Asparagus

Carrots

Brussels sprouts

Eggplant

Yams

Sweet potatoes

Garlic

Ginger

Onions

Peppers (red, green, yellow, jalapeño)

Celery

Zucchini

Tomatoes (heirloom, cherry, grape, etc.)

Mushrooms

Cucumbers

Lettuce (all kinds)

Fruits

Blueberries

Raspberries

Strawberries

Goji berries (these are usually dried)

Grapefruits (ruby red)

Oranges (tangerines, mandarin oranges)

Apples

Bananas

Avocados

Kiwis

Pears

Peaches, nectarines

Plums

Cherries

Melons

Tropical fruits (mango, papaya, pineapple)

Condiments, Drinks, and Dressings

Galeos salad dressing (miso, Dijonnaise, wasabi ginger, Caesar)

Wish-Bone Salad Spritzers

Ground flaxseed

Extra-virgin olive oil

Balsamic vinegar

Pam cooking spray

Mrs. Dash's spices (or any kind of salt-free spice blend)

Mustard (yellow, brown, spicy)

Nonfat mayonnaise

Low-carb barbecue sauce

Low-carb ketchup

Olives (kalamata)

Low-sugar marinara sauce (Colavita)

Tomato paste

Splenda

Green tea

Low-sodium V-8 juice	Coffee
Diet Snapple	No-sugar-added Jell-O
Crystal Light (all flavors)	No-sugar-added Jell-O pudding (chocolate, vanilla)
Arrowhead Sparkling Water (all flavors)	No-sugar-added Popsicles (all kinds)
Diet soda (occasional)	Nabisco 100-calorie snacks

Cooking Tips

As you can see, my food list covers about every kind of food imaginable—except for those nasty processed and packaged foods filled with sodium, nitrates, and other additives that are toxic and make you sick. All that is left are healthy, tasty, rich foods that will please your palate and stomach. Even the foods on my list that come packaged are low in fat and sodium—again the reason behind my choice of brands.

Let's take a look at how to prepare some of these delicious items.

Most of the foods on my list are easy to prepare. In general, for meats, fish, and poultry (proteins), I do a lot of grilling. Of course, you can bake, roast, and even sauté, but quick grilling actually gives the food the most flavor without the risk of added calories through oils.

If you do enjoy meat, fish, or chicken sautéed, then I have two suggestions. The first is to invest in a good-quality sauté pan (either All-Clad or Calphalon); the higher the quality of the pan, the better it cooks. My second suggestion is to use just 1 or 2 teaspoons of olive oil or canola oil. You can also use a cooking spray.

When preparing vegetables, you can grill, steam, or blanch them. Steaming and blanching lock in both flavor and nutrients and don't require added oil. Sometimes I enjoy vegetables raw, which is probably the most healthful way to eat veggies.

Cooking grains, including rice, pasta, and quinoa, usually requires boiling and is therefore very straightforward. Though I have heard of a trick used by some Italian chefs that adding salt to the water not only makes the water boil faster but also locks in the flavor and the starch of the pasta. I doubt there is any science—yet—to support this cooking direction, but you never know!

Legumes are a wonderful source of fiber, but they do tend to be a bit trickier to prepare. Many people avoid cooking beans because they think of the process as time-consuming on account of needing to soak the beans before actually cooking them. You can buy canned beans that simply need to be heated before adding them to a dish. But make sure you do two things: Choose beans without too much added sodium (under 450 milligrams per serving) and rinse them in water. Also, lentils don't require as long to prepare, and they make a delicious alternative to rice or pasta as a side dish.

A Week of Bob's Quick Meals

These meal suggestions are a great way to familiarize yourself with my food list as well as to get comfortable eating in a healthy, satisfying way. None of them takes more than fifteen minutes to prepare and the ingredients are easy to find and assemble.

Breakfast

Option 1

   1 envelope instant weight-control oatmeal

   3 egg whites and 1 whole egg

   Sliced apple

   1½ tablespoons ground flaxseed

Option 2

   Protein scramble (3 egg whites, 1 whole egg, chicken breast, brown rice, black beans) with salsa

Option 3

3 Weetabix squares

1 cup nonfat milk

1 cup fresh berries

2 hard-boiled eggs (throw out one of the yolks)

Sprinkle 1 tablespoon of ground flaxseed on the cereal

Option 4

Protein smoothie (blend 2 scoops of chocolate protein powder, 1 cup nonfat milk, 1 small banana, 1 teaspoon peanut butter, 1 tablespoon ground flaxseed, and ice)

Option 5

1 cup cooked quinoa with mixed berries (strawberries, blueberries, raspberries) or 6–8 raw or dry-roasted almonds

Option 6

1 cup Weetabix Flakes & Fiber Cereal

½ cup nonfat milk

Add berries of choice

2 hardboiled eggs

Option 7

Protein smoothie (blend 1 cup Fage yogurt, ½ cup nonfat milk, ½ cup blueberries, ½ cup raspberries, 1 scoop vanilla protein powder)

Lunch

Option 1

Turkey club (4 ounces low-sodium turkey, 2 strips turkey bacon, lettuce, tomato, 1 slice low-fat cheese, 2 slices whole-wheat bread with a little mustard or nonfat mayo), 1 apple

Option 2

2 grilled chicken breasts, 2 cups steamed broccoli, 1 cup brown rice

Option 3

Large tuna salad (1 can tuna on a large bed of lettuce with tomato, onion, and peppers, 4 tablespoons Galeos wasabi ginger salad dressing, 4 Wasa crackers, 1 cup fresh fruit

Option 4

Turkey burger (turkey burger on a whole-wheat bun with 1 slice of low-fat cheese, lettuce, tomato, mustard, and nonfat mayo), side salad with Galeos salad dressing, 1 apple

Option 5

Tuna salad (1 can tuna, ½ cup cooked quinoa, 2 teaspoons fat-free mayo on mixed greens with 2 teaspoons low-calorie dressing such as Galeo's Dijonnaise)

Option 6

Chicken pasta (4–6 ounces ground chicken breast with low-sugar marinara sauce on top of 1–2 cups brown rice pasta, topped with 1 teaspoon low-fat Parmesan cheese)

Option 7

Fish tacos (4–6 ounces halibut grilled with lemon and Mrs. Dash seasoning, chunky salsa, 1 teaspoon guacamole, and lettuce, wrapped in 2 La Tortilla Factory tortillas)

Dinner

Option 1

Grilled salmon (6 ounces), 2 cups asparagus, side salad, 1 cup no-sugar-added chocolate pudding

Option 2

Fillet of beef (4 ounces), large side salad, 1 small sweet potato, 2 no-sugar-added Popsicles

Option 3

Chicken, beans, and rice (4–6 ounces ground chicken breast, 1 cup black beans, ½ cup low-sugar marinara sauce, over 1 cup brown rice)

Option 4

Grilled red snapper, 2 cups mixed veggies, 1 cup brown rice, 2 no-sugar-added Fudgsicles

Option 5

Steak fajitas (5 ounces grilled beef fillet strips, ¾ cup mixed grilled red peppers and onions, 1 slice avocado, 2 teaspoons salsa, 2 corn tortillas)

Option 6

4–6 ounces grilled ahi tuna, grilled asparagus, large mixed green salad with 2 teaspoons low-calorie dressing

Option 7

Grilled chicken Caesar salad (1–2 grilled chicken breasts, 2–3 cups romaine lettuce, 2 teaspoons low-fat Parmesan cheese, 2–3 Wasa crackers broken up and added to salad as croutons)

Snacks

Option 1

1 tablespoon peanut butter, 1 apple

Option 2

1 cup cottage cheese, 8–10 cherry tomatoes

Option 3

Myoplex Carb Sense protein drink

Option 4

2 Wasa crackers, 2 triangles Laughing Cow Cheese

Option 5

Quesadilla made with ½ cup low-fat mozzarella cheese and 1 tortilla

Option 6

1 cup nonfat yogurt with 1 cup fresh berries

Option 7

2 scoops hummus (preferably organic) in a La Factory tortilla

SIX

Your Food Journal

Your food journal is the place where all of the work you've been doing comes together. As you've moved through the four steps of finding your Inner Compass, you've naturally come to a clearer understanding of yourself, your relationship with food, and your personal goals for achieving weight loss. Now all of that knowledge will guide you as you begin to use your food journal to record not only the foods you eat and when you eat them, but also the feelings you experience as you make your food choices. This record will become your best friend and your road map to success.

The main objective is to help you become accountable for what you are eating during the course of the day. When you actually have to write something down, you are one step closer to becoming more fully responsible for your relationship with food. You can no longer eat on autopilot when you have to write down that handful of M&Ms you inhaled at the office.

Then again, if you decide not to write down everything that you eat and drink, who are you kidding? Only yourself. Basically, the food journal is the fastest, most effective way that I get people to stop lying to themselves. When people become accountable for their own actions, they will feel so much internal power that they will not want to stop.

I don't use anything fancy for my food journal. I simply tear a sheet out of my Filofax agenda that has slots for each hour of the day. But you can use either the two sample pages included here (pages 84 and 85) or whatever form works for you—a spiral notebook, your computer, or even your cell phone if it has note-taking capability!

At first people often find the food journal a nuisance, almost like busywork they can't be bothered with. But when they begin to see the connection between what they are eating and what they are feeling, they begin to take responsibility for themselves at a whole new level. As Joe said, "I don't think I have ever really been so honest with myself." Martha Ann said, "I resisted doing the food journal—it just seemed to take so much time—but now I get it. Everything I do with food is so obvious."

In this way, the food journal becomes your road map to weight loss. You see the impact of food on your moods, the way you think about yourself, and your dips and peaks in confidence. As you become more and more used to being honest with yourself, you begin a new relationship with yourself. As I always point out about two to three weeks into the process, you are becoming your own best friend.

So even though you may at first find the food journal annoying and want to blow it off, you will soon realize that this is your biggest eye-opener. If you have a bad day, you can look back at your food journal for that day or the day before and see if you slipped up somewhere. Many people often will see a connection between straying from their healthy eating plan and feeling a dip in how they feel, losing a sense of balance and well-being. Like any new friendship, you need to start with honesty and reliability. Once you start truly connecting with yourself at a conscious level, the whole world opens up to you. Again, when you're able to see yourself in the third person and watch yourself through the course of your day, you begin to see when those thoughts start coming up: "I'm fat, I'm stupid." By recognizing your daily routine, you become conscious of your triggers. And instead of eating to block out a painful feeling, you now have the power to say, "Oh, there's that devil on my shoulder saying that I'm never going to get that promotion or that I will never meet anyone. Hi there, you little devil." In acknowledging the voice, you take away the voice's authority. Then the voice becomes smaller, and it no longer has the power to drive your decisions. This is how the changes begin to happen. You are in charge because you have taken charge.

Your Calorie Goal: 1500 calories   **Date:** 8/12/07

Today's Weight: 186 pounds   **How You Feel Today:**

Meal	Time	Food	Calories	Feeling
Breakfast	7 A.M.	1 cup cold cereal	145	
		1 cup blueberries	60	
		1 cup skim milk	90	
		1 banana	110	
		TOTAL	405	
Lunch	11:30 A.M.	Lean chicken breast, grilled	110	
		1 cup raw carrots	50	
		Lettuce	60	
		TOTAL	344	
Snack	3 P.M.	Chocolate bar	250	guilty
Dinner	6 P.M.	1 cup whole-wheat pasta	109	
		½ cup spinach with garlic	240	
		2 cups tossed salad	40	
		½ cup tomato sauce	35	
		1 cup mixed fruit	240	
		TOTAL	664	
		DAILY TOTAL FOR CALORIES	1413	

Your Thoughts Today:

I started the day really well and was feeling good about myself, but by the time I reached 3:00 I felt famished. I knew I shouldn't have eaten that chocolate bar, but I ate it anyway and felt so guilty right after. I always try and remember what Bob has told me—that if I make a mistake or a bad food choice, just get back on the horse again. I try not to be hard on myself for cheating. Dinner was much better and I know tomorrow I will do even better. So far, I've lost 13 pounds in four weeks.

Bob's Response:

A chocolate bar is a chocolate bar. Don't get stuck in your guilty feeling. In fact, take a minute to remember exactly how you were feeling right before you went into that store to buy the candy (because I know it wasn't in your purse, car, or cupboard at home). Were you feeling tired from a long day at work? For most of my clients 3 or 4 P.M. is the witching hour, when their energy level plummets and they are feeling rather frantic for a quick pick-me-up. Sugar is definitely going to give you a boost, but it will wear off quickly. A better snack is a handful of nuts, such as raw almonds, or an energy bar if you are really hungry and your lunch was light—but watch the calories on the label of that bar, especially its fat content! I try to keep nuts with me at all times—it doesn't take more than a handful to feel the energy you're looking for.

Your Calorie Goal: **Date:**

Today's Weight: **How You Feel Today:**

Meal	Time	Food	Calories	Feeling
Breakfast				
		TOTAL		
Lunch				
		TOTAL		
Snack				
Dinner				
		TOTAL		
		DAILY TOTAL FOR CALORIES		

Your Thoughts Today:

Maximizing the Value of Your Food Journal

Your food journal can be your road map to health. You can use it to record not only what and when you eat but how you are feeling. As you know by this point, it's quite easy to turn to food when you're feeling stressed by life events or you find yourself feeling overwhelmed and confused by your emotions. When you worked through the four steps of the Inner Compass plan, you began to see and understand your relationship with food, but you also probably gained insight into how you use food. As you pay more attention to how you think and feel and begin to make healthy food choices, you may also want to keep in mind some strategies for making this eating plan work best for you.

Create a Schedule

As with any change in your life, you may feel a bit unsettled at first, which is why I keep a lot of familiar foods on the meal plan. I don't want to take you too far away from your comfort zone, or I know you will be tempted to throw in the towel. One of the best ways to get in a groove is by creating a schedule of when you plan to eat. This will help you manage your anxiety about when your next meal will come.

Plan Your Meals

If you shop once a week, take time before you head to the store to plan out most of your meals for the upcoming week. Like scheduling your meals, planning what they will consist of will help manage any nervousness that you may feel as you begin to change your diet.

Revisit Your Goals

Back in Chapter Three, I asked you to write down your goals. Do you want to lose 20 pounds, 50 pounds, 100 pounds? Now that you know more about food, calories, and how to lose weight, you may want to revisit your goals to make sure they are realistic. Instead of planning on losing 50 pounds in six months, maybe it's more realistic to expect this loss of weight to happen over a year's time, at a pound a week.

If you're impatient and want to see results sooner, then know that it's possible to increase the amount of weight you can lose per week, but you will have to watch your calories more strictly and make sure you are exercising at least four to five times a week (you will find out much more about how exercise boosts weight loss in Part 3).

You can tailor my eating and fitness plan to work for you, both immediately and in the long term. Either way, it adapts to your short-term and long-term goals and enables you to maintain your desired weight forever.

Weigh Yourself

I am of two minds about weighing yourself. On one hand, weighing yourself on a daily basis helps you keep track of how you are eating, especially if you see a jump of a pound or two or an unyielding plateau. If you are weighing yourself, you can catch yourself, figure out what to do about it, and get yourself back on track.

However, it's easy for the scale to become something you obsess about. If you're constantly running to the scale to check your weight, then you are not relaxing, enjoying your food, and engaged in your life.

So here's my advice: Weigh yourself, but do so in moderation. Weigh yourself in the morning with no or few clothes on and always use the same scale. Keep in mind that as you integrate exercise into your life, specifically strength training, you will gain muscle mass, and muscle weighs more than fat. So a plateau on the scale may be an indication that you are losing fat and gaining muscle, which is not a bad thing. In fact, the more muscular you are, the more fat you burn!

I can't remind you enough to keep a record of the foods you are eating throughout the day. This is especially important when you are in the early stages of this program. If you keep track of your foods and your feelings, then you will understand why you feel good and why you feel not so good. Yes, I know it takes time. But think about how much attention you are giving to yourself—in this way, the food journal is a daily way of saying, "I'm important." Even if you have a bad day and stray from my food list or eat too much, if you are writing it all down, then you are still taking care of yourself. By simply being honest with yourself and your food choices, you have stepped away from unconscious eating and toward a place of fuller responsibility. This is the essence of taking charge of your life!

SEVEN

Stress Busters

There's no doubt about it: Our lives are filled with stress. It's an inevitable, unavoidable part of daily living. One of the ways the body reacts to stress is by releasing cortisol through the adrenal glands. When our adrenal glands are overworked, a by-product of our always feeling like we're in fight-or-flight mode, our cortisol level is always elevated. The danger of this? Belly fat. It's scary but true: Stress can make us fat.

Although we may feel powerless to prevent stress from creeping into our lives, we are not powerless to cope with it. This chapter will focus on ways you can cope with or manage stress more wisely and efficiently, so that you can regain control and not let stress take over your life. You can stay focused and comfortable in your eating plan, and you will.

My clients and participants in *The Biggest Loser* also find it helpful to know what to do when they travel, go on vacation, or attend holiday parties or other social events. Fast-food restaurants are everywhere, which means that temptations are everywhere. When you learn how to order from a drive-through menu, then you will no longer feel that the golden arches have power over you—instead, you will be in charge. You will find specific tips on how to navigate all of life's obstacles so that you remain in charge!

The Chemistry of Stress

Our bodies are hardwired for stress. Our flight-or-fight reflex is a built-in response to danger nearby. Obviously, we don't live in constant danger from predators in the same way that our ancestors did, but our bodies often react to stress as if we did. Our heart rate goes up, our muscles tense, and we become hyperaware. Also, our adrenal glands release a hormone called cortisol, and as I mentioned above, chronically high levels of cortisol can result in excess fat storage, especially around our bellies.

Although researchers are looking into drugs and supplements that may help regulate our bodies' cortisol production, a better, safer way to combat cortisol release is by managing how you react to stress. First and foremost, you need to become more attuned to what causes you stress and what enables you to relax. The more you pay attention to this connection, the better you can manage the stress by putting in place coping strategies.

For example, let's say you begin to feel more and more anxious as you head into the holiday season, as many of us do. The holidays may remind you of unhappy days growing up or the isolation and loneliness you may feel in your life at this time, but regardless of the cause, we can often feel an increase in stress. If you know this about yourself, you can offset the impact of stress by turning to activities or tools that keep both your mind and body in a more relaxed state.

What relaxes us varies greatly. Me, I love to exercise—hard. I run, hike, or lift weights. Working out has always been a stress reliever. But other people, who may not get off on pushing their bodies in the same way, can achieve the same results by doing what they enjoy. Maybe it's a walk in the neighborhood with the dog. Or maybe you sit down with a cup of tea and call a friend for a long chat. Perhaps what relaxes you is meditation or prayer. It's really up to you to figure out what helps you to relax so that when a stressful situation arises, you can turn to one of these activities as a way to ease the feelings of anxiety.

Learning good coping skills is key to managing the inevitable stresses of our lives. As our mothers tried to do for us when we were babies, we are teaching ourselves how to comfort and soothe ourselves. The more capable we are at doing this, the more confident we are that we can handle almost anything—especially a lifestyle change that is so good for us.

Dining Out and Eating on the Go

Face it, we are a culture that loves to eat out—at restaurants, at fast-food joints, and even in our cars! It seems we eat anywhere but at home at the dining room table. So even though my food list is easy to use, I know that many of you have to dine out occasionally or even on a regular basis.

When you do so, there are some tips you should keep in mind:

- Choose restaurants that you know serve some fresh foods, including salads and grilled meats and chicken.

- Don't be shy about asking the kitchen to prepare a food without oil or salt. Remember, oil adds fat calories and salt makes you want them.

- Always ask the waiter for your dressing to be served on the side so you can choose the amount to put on your salad.

- Refrain from eating bread—you may even want to ask the waiter not to bring it to the table.

- Eat your salad before your meal. This way, you fill up on fiber-rich greens and will eat less carbs and protein.

- If the portions are enormous—and they tend to be in this country—decide what amount you will eat and then push the rest to the side of your plate and bring it home.

- Instead of ordering an entrée, choose one or two appetizers. This way, you can still enjoy the experience of dining in a restaurant, but you avoid overindulging in richer foods than you would prepare for yourself at home.

- Choose fruit for dessert. Yes, it's hard to resist finishing off a meal with something sweet, but instead of selecting a high-fat, high-sugar food, satisfy your taste buds with a fruit cup or sorbet that will cleanse your palate and answer the call for something sweet.

When you need to stop at a convenience store or eat at a fast-food restaurant, educate yourself on their fresh, lower-calorie meals. Essentially all the fast-food chains now offer non-fried options that are lower in calories. For instance, many of my clients rave about the salads at McDonald's and Wendy's. And all of the chains offer grilled chicken options. Taco Bell even offers fajitas. But remember, choose the soft flour taco rather than the fried hard shell.

One of my favorite fast-food options is Subway, which offers a great selection of sandwiches with a limited amount of calories. They also fill their sandwiches with nutritious, crunchy vegetables that add flavor, fiber, and texture, making the whole eating experience that much more enjoyable and satisfying.

If you can't resist a burger craving, then go for it, but take off the cheese (that saves you at least 120 calories), avoid special sauces, and make the burger "topless"—eat only one side of the bun. Or you can wrap the burger in lettuce and forget the bun entirely.

A harder pill to swallow is my request that you stay away from french fries. I know what you are going to say, but please, I am begging you: Resist the fries! They are not only high in calories but also almost always filled with trans fat that practically blocks your arteries upon ingestion. If your craving for fries is uncontrollable, then you absolutely must purchase the smallest size.

A general guideline when eating at a fast-food restaurant is to avoid anything fried. You also want to avoid chips, packaged candy, baked goods such as donuts, and other high-starch or high-sugar foods that contain saturated fat, trans fat, and additives that are unhealthy.

Travel

We are also a nation of travelers. But no longer is travel a carefree experience filled with frills. Long gone are the days when you were served a plentiful meal atop a tray with a white napkin! Traveling by plane, in particular, is an anxiety-inducing, chaotic mess, which makes it even more important that you take good care of yourself—before, during, and after your trip. My first piece of advice is to never let yourself get hungry. The best way to avoid getting hungry is by bringing food along with you. I fly a lot, and I always have my trusty bag of nuts with me. Some of you may enjoy a low-calorie energy bar, but make sure you check the label—some of these energy bars are loaded with unnecessary fat and sugar. You also want to choose snacks that travel well (i.e., don't need refrigeration) and are fiber-rich.

If you know you are going on a very long flight, or multiple flights, try to bring a sandwich or some other meal with you. Fresh fruit, nuts, and raisins are great healthy snacks. Of course, you also want to drink plenty of water, but as you probably know, you need to purchase your water after you go through security clearance.

Life's a Party

Family gatherings, social events, and holidays are prime time for indulgences. When it's time to party, it's easy to lose sight of your goals, relax, and have too good a time. Now, I'm not saying you have to restrict yourself. I actually think enjoying an indulgence or two is good for both body and soul. But as I've said earlier, straying too far away from your eating plan can be a slippery slope.

Here are some tips that can keep you free and clear of that downhill course:

- Eat before you go. If you arrive at a party or event on an empty stomach, you are much more likely to eat what is being served . . . and those options are often going to be fatty.

- Limit your alcohol intake. Not only are wine, beer, and mixed drinks filled with calories, the alcohol will wear away your resolve.

- If you're attending a family event, offer to bring a dish that you know is low in fat and/or calories and that you will enjoy eating.

- During holiday time, decide ahead of time how long you will be staying at the party.

Shopping Strategies

As you become familiar with the foods on my food list and begin to decide on recipes, including those in my list of quick meals, you may need to shop a bit differently. Your grocery store may not carry some of the brands I am recommending, or it may not have enough fresh produce and meat options.

If not, then you may need to research your options and find other sources for your shopping.

You may also need to approach shopping in a different manner. Here's what I have found to be helpful to many clients:

- Plan most of your big meals at the beginning of each week, and make a list of the ingredients you need to purchase.

- Prior to going to the store, make a list of what you need.

- Never shop hungry.

- Don't overbuy.

- Try to buy local, fresh, or organic ingredients when possible.

- Keep fresh fruits and vegetables on hand so that when you want a late-night snack, you have something healthy to reach for.

- Stock up on frozen fruits and vegetables, especially when they are out of season.

- Stay away from canned goods, as often they contain a high amount of sodium. However, I often buy canned beans and legumes (lentils, chickpeas, beans, etc.), but I rinse them with water before cooking to wash away the excess sodium.

- Avoid buying junk food—chips, candy, ice cream, popcorn. If it's in your cupboard or freezer, you will feel more tempted to indulge.

Staying the Course

Again, before you begin your eating plan, it is important to create meaningful, achievable goals. You also need to be honest with yourself. What do you weigh now? What do you want to weigh? (See page 41 for a guide to determining your ideal weight.)

If you have any health issues, I also recommend that you check in with your physician or health care professional and share your plan to begin this program. He or she may also be helpful in determining your goals—in terms of not only weight loss but also your overall health. Keep in mind that many of my clients have not only reversed their long-term disease symptoms and conditions but also gotten off their medications and freed themselves of the medications' side effects.

Here is a quick checklist to use as you begin:

1. Determine how much you weigh, how much you want to lose, and approximately how long that will take you.

2. Go over the information on page 60 about the basics of nutrition. The more you know about enhancing your nutritional intake, the better the choices you will make about food.

3. Set aside time each day to check in with yourself. How are you feeling? Have you noticed any major or subtle changes in how you are thinking about yourself since beginning the diet? Do you take time each day for yourself just to relax? When you truly relax, you help your mind let go and rest.

4. Use the food journal pages to keep track of your progress by recording your weight and the foods you are eating throughout the day. Your journal is an important part of becoming conscious and aware of the healthy habits of your new lifestyle.

5. Review the food list and familiarize yourself with the foods you will be eating. Also, take a look at my quick meal suggestions and see which appeal to you. You may need to revise your grocery list.

6. Get used to planning ahead of time some if not all of your meals in the initial weeks of following my eating plan. This will help you have the right foods on hand when you get hungry. Hunger and tempting foods make for bad decisions!

As you merge your heart, mind, and body and give all that you are to optimizing your health, remember to love yourself and to be your own best friend. Remember to cherish your body and treat it with respect. Remember to reinforce your confidence and acknowledge your accomplishments. Remember that by taking responsibility for your health, you are not only serving yourself but giving back to others—for now you have the power to do so.

PART 3

My Workout

You are *so* ready to take charge of your life—from the inside out! In Part 1, you learned how to take control of your Inner Compass, redirecting your energy, your focus, and your goals. This internal work automatically will make you feel stronger and more confident. And as you begin to follow the eating plan, soon you will feel lighter, leaner, and more nimble from eating clean, nutrient-dense food and taking out the fatty, sugary foods that weigh down both your body and your mind. The final piece to integrate is exercise that will maximize both your weight loss and your overall fitness.

As you do your Inner Compass work and change your way of eating, I am also asking that you begin my fitness program. Like my eating plan, my fitness plan is simple. It's meant to be a lifestyle, not a complicated routine that wears away resolve and builds boredom. Rather, you learn how to incorporate exercise into your daily and weekly routine gradually, so that it becomes as natural—and as necessary—as breathing.

My fitness plan works in two phases. Phase One begins with four weeks of pure cardio. In this phase, you will once and for all learn how to make exercise part of your lifestyle. In fact, this is the single most valuable lesson you can take away from my approach to getting in shape. When exercise becomes a regular part of your routine, not only do you feel better and look better, you find that you miss it when you don't do it.

I recommend that everyone, whether you've never done any exercise or you're a former Marine and current triathlete, begin with Phase One for four weeks. This coincides with the initial period of both your Inner Compass work and your eating plan.

In Phase Two, I expand the pure cardio of Phase One by adding strengtheners with specific circuit training and core challenge routines. In Phase Two you will be encouraged to work out on five days, alternating pure cardio (on two days) with three days of circuit training and core challenge routines that integrate a cardio component as they strengthen your upper and lower body and core.

For Phase Two, when you add strengtheners to your workout, I have designed a number of different combination routines that target all areas of your body, including upper and lower muscle groups, your core (the muscles in your abdomen), and your overall body, so that as you increase the intensity and duration of your workout, you tone and hone your mental and physical shape and increase your weight loss. All the exercises I suggest have built-in modifications and levels of ease or difficulty. So if you've never done a leg lift, never mind lifted a barbell, take a deep breath and relax. I'm going to show you how to get started in a safe, gradual way that will not rip you out of your comfort zone (that comes later—just kidding). As you know, my opening mantra is "Relax." And even when you start getting your heart pumping with a twenty-minute walk, you will do so in a relaxed state of mind.

All the exercises are accompanied by photos and diagrams, and you can do them in the comfort of your own home. They also require minimal equipment and space. You will see that I have provided equipment lists—a list of basics and a list of ideals. If you're new to this game, then I suggest starting with the basics—nothing costs more than $25. If you're really strapped for cash, then you can do without the equipment for a while.

Again, all of the exercises include variations geared toward your individual fitness level. The more familiar you are with a particular movement and the more proficient you become, the more likely you will be to challenge yourself in intensity and duration.

You want to make sure that you don't strain your "soft spots," those places on your body that are most prone to injury, including your neck, back, and knees. Making slight adjustments in your stance and posture, as well as becoming more aware of your body in space, can do wonders to avoid pulling something out of whack.

Some of you may already have a workout that you enjoy and rely on to keep you in shape and help you manage your weight. If that's the case, there is a lot in the following pages and chapters that will help you further strengthen and tone certain areas of your body and create more lean muscle mass. You'll also find some fun cardio challenges to add to your routine that will increase your metabolism as well as improve your overall health. It's this combination—cardio and strength training—that will increase and cement your weight loss.

Now let's get started!

EIGHT

Getting Started

— Phase One —

I was so afraid to even begin moving my body, but now that I'm two weeks into it, I can't believe it took me so long to get into working out. It makes me feel so alive!" says Erin, who has now been working out for three months and has lost 10 pounds. Arielle, a former Marine, had once been very fit, able to handle the physical and mental challenges of long obstacle courses and other military training exercises. But by the time she joined *The Biggest Loser,* she had gained 75 pounds and hadn't been physically active in almost five years. What was her motivation to get fit? "I had just lost a sense of myself. But the idea of getting back into shape was overwhelming."

That's right. Getting started is as much a mental activity as it is a physical activity. When working with my regular clients as well as the contestants on *The Biggest Loser,* I always have them begin in a way that doesn't send their entire lives into a tailspin. Exercise is meant to be fun, not punishment. You're meant to enjoy it, look forward to it, and appreciate it—not just because it makes you look better but because you feel so much better in your body. Like changing your diet from one that is filled with fatty, processed foods to one that is clean, nutritious, and pleasing to the palate, getting your body into shape will make you feel lighter, leaner, and stronger. You will also grow in confidence and develop a stronger sense of self.

As you read the pages that follow, keep in mind that you everyone starts somewhere, and as you learned from your Inner Compass work, you need to accept your starting point, be patient with yourself, and remind yourself of every single accomplishment you achieve along the way.

Why Exercise?

By now, most of us are familiar with the knowledge that exercising on a regular basis increases weight loss. But did you realize that it's been scientifically proven that regular physical activity substantially reduces the risk of dying of coronary heart disease, the nation's leading cause of death? Or that it also decreases the risk of stroke, colon cancer, diabetes, and high blood pressure—all of which plague our nation of overweight people? Regular exercise also helps keep our bones solid and our muscles and joints strong and flexible, helps relieve the pain of arthritis, and has the power to offset anxiety and depression.

My workout is designed to do all of these things and more. Its three phases are designed to:

- Increase your heart's and lungs' stamina

- Make your muscles strong and able to sustain activity for a long time without tiring

- Redistribute your weight so you add lean muscle mass and decrease fat, making your body able to burn more calories even when resting

- Increase your flexibility, which allows for the comfortable movement of your muscles, bones, and joints, especially as you age

You will be doing both upper-body and lower-body routines that focus on muscle strengthening through weights and resistance training. And when you repeat the suggested combinations, you add in a cardio element, thereby increasing your endurance and stamina. You will also learn how to increase your range of motion, making yourself more flexible. Good flexibility in the joints can help prevent injuries through all stages of life.

As you begin this two-phase plan, you will begin to experience an increase in energy, see a tightening of your skin and tissue as fat turns into muscle, and feel yourself getting lighter and leaner. This workout is proven to do it all for you!

The Two Phases: A View from Above

As I mention above, my fitness plan is a two-phase workout that begins with Phase One, designed for everyone, at every fitness level. At first, this approach may not make sense to you—how can someone who has never exercised before or who hasn't exercised in years follow the same plan as someone who is already running thirty minutes at a stretch or who is used to weight lifting or yoga? The answer lies in how my fitness plan is designed to last a lifetime. The two phases are not meant to be a twelve-week plan that you move through as levels only to complete at the end of those three months. Rather, you will move in and out of the phases for the rest of your life.

So yes, everyone starts with Phase One (four weeks of pure cardio) and progresses to Phase Two by adding in circuit training and core challenges at varying levels of intensity and duration. You will see that the first time you work through Phase Two, you are focused mostly on learning the exercises, relearning how your body moves, and getting your mind and body in sync. Once you become familiar with the routines, then you are better able to increase the number of repetitions, the weights, and the duration of time you spend doing the routines.

If you find you have a few weeks of extra stress or complications in your life, you may choose to go back and do Phase One exclusively for a week or two. The simplicity of Phase One is refreshing and revitalizing and can be a great way to calm your mind and body. I often resort to Phase One alone when I am feeling overly stressed (who, me?)—it works wonders to ground me in myself and get me back to a healthy perspective on all that I have going on in my life.

Then there are those times when I love the challenge and intensity of Phase Two and get into revving up my body with the different workouts (I provide you with three workout options). I may do it for a month or two, then slow down and return to pure cardio again.

The point is this: Like my eating plan, my fitness plan is a lifestyle that you control. Once again, you are in charge!

Listening to Your Body

Many trainers offer only one way to do their workouts. Not me. I believe that the only way a workout will stick and the only way people will truly make exercise part of their lifestyle is if they own their workout. That said, it's very important that you pay attention to your body and how it is responding to the new movements and the rigor of a cardio workout.

The more you pay attention to how you feel during a workout (and after), the more accustomed you will become to deciding how hard to push yourself and when to move from Phase One to Phase Two. Although most people move from Phase One to Phase Two after four weeks, some of you may want to linger with the pure cardio because of its simplicity or because your body is still adapting to movement, especially if you have never exercised before. By all means, stick with it. When you are very comfortable with your cardio routine, whether that is straight walking, running, or working out on a treadmill, Stairmaster, or other cardio machine, and you want to see more visible results with your body, then you are ready to add the strengtheners and circuit training elements.

Your Heart Rate

Another way to determine whether you are ready to move into Phase Two is by checking your heart rate. If your heart rate decreases in the four-week span, then you have clear, concrete evidence that your body is becoming more fit and you are ready to move on to the next phase, which will make your body even stronger and more fit. There are many heart rate monitors available, some fancy, complicated, and expensive, others very simple and inexpensive, such as those put out by Polar. Or you can track your heart rate by placing a finger (not the thumb) on the opposite wrist at the pulse point, which is below the base of the thumb. For some people it's easier to find their pulse by placing their index finger or index and middle fingers under the back of their jawbone. To check your resting heart rate, count the number of heartbeats in ten seconds and multiply by 6. This is your resting heart rate per minute. Do the same right after you finish your cardio workout.

Perceived Level of Exertion

Some people know they are ready to move from one phase to the next when they have an overall sensory feeling that they need more. This feeling is often described by trainers as the "perceived level of exertion." As this phrase suggests, only you can really determine how hard your body is working during exercise.

However, to help you get used to paying attention to how your body feels and determine when and if you are ready to challenge it a bit more, you may want to use a standard scale of perceived exertion defined by the world-renowned trainer Gunnar Borg. I have adapted these ten levels to distinguish how hard you experience your body working. Here are the ten levels:

1. *No exertion at all.* You feel no real effort and are barely paying attention to your workout.

2. *Very easy.* This would be the way you feel if you were moving around your kitchen or bedroom, moving but not really working out.

3. *Somewhat easy.* This is how you might feel as you begin to move your body at the beginning of a workout, when doing the five-minute warm-up.

4. *Moderate.* You feel okay, but you can definitely notice your heart pumping harder and you may begin to break a sweat.

5. *Moderately difficult.* Now you are definitely breaking a sweat, and you have created a rhythm as your heart beats harder.

6. *Hard.* Your breathing is now more intense, but you don't feel stressed.

7. *Very hard.* If you move from a walk to a run, or if you change to a heavier weight, you will begin to feel a bit more labored breathing and may even feel some muscle fatigue.

8. *Extremely hard.* This is the level of a vigorous workout; it may be difficult for you to have a conversation.

9. *Extremely difficult.* This level feels very strenuous, like you are approaching your maximum. Your breathing is deep and hard and you really can't carry on a conversation.

10. *Maximal exertion.* This level is the most physically intense that you can attain; even very few athletes reach such a peak.

If you have never exercised before beginning this program, then I would keep your level of exertion to between 3 and 5. After the four-week mark, if the same cardio workout feels easier (say, you rate it a 2 or 3 now instead of a 4 or 5, as when you began it), then you are ready to move on to Phase Two.

However, if after four weeks the pure cardio workout of a twenty- or thirty-minute walk still makes you feel like it's a level 4 or 5, then I recommend that you stay with another two to four weeks of pure cardio.

If you have exercised in the past but not in a year or two, or if you are used to very moderate exercise once in a while, then you need to make sure your pure cardio workout gets you to 4 or 5 right away. If walking doesn't do this, then try something a bit more challenging, such as walking on an inclined treadmill or doing a light run. And remember, it's not about the distance; it's about the time.

Essentially, as you progress beyond four weeks of starting the fitness plan, any workout (unless you're a world-class athlete) should fall between levels 4 and 7.

The perceived levels of exertion are just that—perceived. So they rely very much on you paying close attention to how you feel. If you feel really winded one day, then back off. If you have a lot going on in your life, stress may make a typical workout more strenuous. Pay attention!

What You Need

Equipment

To start Phase One of the fitness plan, all you need is one thing: a pair of good running shoes. You may already have a pair of running shoes. They may be worn, even a bit tattered. You might think you don't even *deserve* a new pair. But you do. Treat yourself to a new pair as you begin this Fitness Plan; let the new shoes be a gift to yourself, representing your new beginning.

As you proceed and begin the workout, integrating the strengtheners (the resistance-training exercises) of your upper and lower body, as well as the core challenge exercises in Phase Two, you may want to invest in some minimal equipment. Again, these are not necessary for a good workout, but many people find these items an easy way to increase the challenge and add variety.

The Basics

All the basic pieces of equipment cost less than $25 each.

- Rubber band

- 1–3 sets of free (hand) weights, in 3-, 5-, 10-, and 15-pound weights

- Jump rope

- Physio ball—these come in two sizes, 55 centimeters for people 5'3"–5'7" and 65 centimeters for people 5'9" and above

The Ideals

The ideals are a bit more pricey, but some can be found in a gym, if you belong to one.

- Bosu ball (about $75)

- Mat (yoga style or other)

- Step or bench

- Gym equipment. Most of us do not own one of these larger pieces of workout equipment, but if you are a member of a gym, it's a good idea to familiarize yourself with these machines as you proceed from Phase One to Phase Two.

  – Treadmill

  – Stairmaster

  – Elliptical trainer

  – Stationary bike

Phase One: Pure Cardio

In Phase One, I am asking you to walk, simply because you can. This activity requires the least amount of preparation and equipment and offers the greatest amount of ease. The focus and end result of Phase One is making this routine an automatic part of your daily and weekly schedule so that both your brain and your body will come to expect and need this physical activity. Soon you will be moving with greater ease and satisfaction. Soon you will need and want to move more rigorously and for longer periods of time. Soon you will say to yourself, "I can do this!"

I ask you to stay in Phase One for at least four weeks. This is not an arbitrary period; rather, it's based on science that has shown it takes the brain three to four weeks to create a new habit. What you are doing by following this routine is laying a new neural pathway that essentially hardwires your body and brain for physical activity.

So if you have never followed an exercise routine or program, if you haven't moved your body through space with the intention of raising your heart rate and flexing your muscles, then not only will you learn to do so but you will come to enjoy—and need—this exercise.

Here are the four things you must do in Phase One. Again, this phase is all about cardio.

1. Set aside at least twenty to thirty minutes three or four days a week. This is your "me time," the time each day you give yourself. You may have been using this time to keep your food journal; you may

even have taken some of my other suggestions and begun to meditate or do some other mind-body work. Now you are going to use this "me time" to get your body moving.

2. Establish a schedule. Most people begin on Monday and work out on Monday, Wednesday, and Friday. Others choose to begin on Tuesday and work out on Tuesday, Thursday, and Saturday. If you begin to add a fourth day, then shift your schedule to Monday, Wednesday, Friday, and Sunday, or Tuesday, Thursday, Saturday, and Monday. The idea is to give yourself a break in between your cardio workouts.

3. Use this time to walk. Walk on your treadmill, walk around your neighborhood, or do the stairs. If you are extremely uncomfortable moving, then simply get up, walk to your mailbox, and walk back. Then do it again. If you need to sit down in between trips, then take a rest. Just move for twenty to thirty minutes, three or four days each week. If you are going to a gym, then familiarize yourself with the cardio equipment, such as the elliptical machine, the stationary bike, or the stepper (Stairmaster).

4. Create a routine. If you take these two steps—setting aside the time and making your body move—three or four days per week, then you have in effect established a routine. It is this routine, this plan, this expectation of yourself that is going to give you the power to change the nature of your relationship with exercise.

Finding Your Cardio Zone

Cardio fitness is an important part of getting in shape and improving your overall health. Any exercise that is aerobic, in which you increase the amount of oxygen you take in and your heart pumps more blood, improves not only your cardiovascular health but your level of fitness as well as helping you lose weight.

You may want to increase the duration of your cardio workout from thirty minutes to forty minutes; you may want to increase your frequency from three or four days to four, five, or six days. Play around with your routine, but don't break it.

Most of you will be ready to move from Phase One to Phase Two at the end of the four-week period. If, however, you are really enjoying the simplicity of the walking routine as you pursue the eating plan and your Inner Compass work, then by all means stick with the walking. But you will get faster results if you add in Phase Two.

Remember, Phase One coincides with the most intense part of your new eating plan. When you begin walking and changing the way you eat, you will start to see the weight drop off and your energy return. But you will probably feel intense fatigue at times. This is all normal. In fact, your body and mind both require more rest and sleep now. You have to be gentle and patient with yourself. Change is always stressful and requires more mental and emotional energy.

As I state above, when you first begin my program, the main goal is to get your body moving while establishing a routine and setting aside time in your daily and weekly schedule to make sure you exercise. So I recommend that for the first four weeks of being on the eating plan, all you do is walk. Are you a morning person? Then walk in the morning. Get up a half hour earlier, cut out your TV news viewing or newspaper reading, and walk instead. Are you a night person and think you will enjoy walking at the end of the day? Then walk at the end of the day. Or fit it in on your lunch break. All I'm asking at this point is that you walk twenty minutes three to five days per week. You can always find twenty minutes to walk.

If you want to challenge yourself further in Phase One, then you can run, walk on an inclined treadmill, or do the Stairmaster or any other form of cardio that you enjoy. If you are running or doing anything more than walking, make sure to treat the first five minutes of your workout as a warm-up, letting your muscles warm up before exerting yourself fully. For example, if you are going to run for thirty minutes, start by walking or jogging slowly for five minutes. Then increase your pace. Walking, jogging, swimming, and cycling are all examples of good cardio workouts. Aerobic activity can involve any type of exercise that raises your metabolism and gets your heart beating a bit faster—even gardening, performing household chores such as vacuuming, and of course taking the stairs instead of the elevator.

As you will see in Chapters Nine and Ten, I've designed many of my strength-training routines to provide a cardio workout as well. So once you are ready to start focusing on your upper and lower body, you will increase your cardio fitness even more.

CARDIO OPTIONS GALORE

Anything that makes your heart pump is a cardio workout. Consider these:

Spin class

Train for a 5K walk or run

Swimming

Tennis

Racquetball

Water aerobics

Hiking

It's Up to You

For some people, Phase One is the hardest—not because the exercise itself is strenuous but because they are adapting to this new routine. We are all creatures of habit, and when we make any change in our daily or weekly routine, we feel it. But soon your workout will become not only a reliable part of your day but a "must" on your to-do list.

If you're eating fewer unhealthy foods, you're eating every four hours from my food list, and you have begun walking twenty minutes per day three to five times a week, then you no doubt will begin seeing and feeling a change in your body. As Linda said, "I never thought walking would help me lose weight. It's so simple, but I've already lost 10 pounds in two months of walking three times a week for twenty minutes!"

It's not a miracle. It's common sense. You are eating less and exercising more; that is the key to any kind of weight loss. Weight loss is happening—and not just in terms of pounds of flesh, but in mental pounds of worry and tension. You feel lighter because your heart is working more efficiently. Your blood is pumping through your veins more strongly.

Again, if you are very new to exercising or you find it difficult to get yourself motivated or stick to any form of aerobic exercise, the best place to start is walking slowly and steadily, giving yourself a lot of time to gradually progress to a faster-paced walk. "I love walking," said Paul, who lost more than 35 pounds over the course of six months. "It doesn't even feel like exercise." You may even surprise yourself and get to the point where you actually enjoy going jogging or running. But remember, in order for it to be effective, you have to do your cardio workout regularly.

And remember the three Rs:

- *Relax*. Give yourself a break when you need it.

- *Respect*. Listen to your body; if you need a rest or a break, then take it. Some injuries can be prevented this way.

- *Reinforce*. Acknowledge the progress you are making so that you reinforce your commitment to taking care of yourself.

John, who had discovered the power of keeping the food journal early on, said this about starting a regular walking routine: "I never knew how good walking could feel. Just moving my body and getting outside has been huge! I feel so much better!" Remember, this is your "me time," the time you have set aside to take care of yourself. The more regularly you allow for this time, the more you will discover that you absolutely need it. In fact, you can't do without it.

NINE

My Master List

Before you can follow the phases easily and efficiently, it's important that you familiarize yourself with the individual exercises. That way, when you are ready to start your workout, you'll know ahead of time what you will be doing. Below is what I call my master list, which includes all of the exercises and all of the adjustments and variations, as well as photos illustrating how to do the movements.

Eventually, you will know these exercises by heart—you will even get to a place of such familiarity that you will be able to mix and match from the four major categories of movement to create your own workout. But for now, you need to get acquainted with how to do them correctly and in a way that does not cause injury.

Push/Pull Exercises

Push/pull exercises focus on opening, toning, and strengthening your shoulders, upper back, and chest. Here are my favorites.

Push-up/Pull-up

You're going to need your hand weights for this movement. Here we will combine movement concentrating on your chest and your back, but once you start doing this, you will realize that the whole body is being utilized.

1. Grip your hand weights and get in a push-up position, with your weights just below your chest. Be sure not to have your hands/weights out too far in front of you.

2. Keeping your shoulders down and away from your ears, and your core strength strong (your abdominal muscles), bring the chest down into a push-up position.

3. On the way up, add the pull-up, bringing the weight in your right hand up toward your underarms, elbow brushing your side.

4. Place the weight back down in the original position and repeat with the left arm.

That was one rep.

Step 1:
Push-up position with weights below your chest.

Step 2:
Lower down.

Step 3:
Push into weighted right hand and raise left hand with bent elbow.

Step 4:
Repeat on other side.

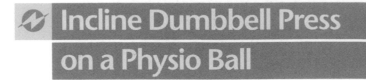

Incline Dumbbell Press on a Physio Ball

1. Hold your weights above your chest with your arms slightly bent and weights facing each other.

2. Keep your elbows in the same position as you lower the weights down just level with your chest, pause for a second, then bring the weights back up.

Step 1:
Starting position.

Step 2:
Raise your arms.

Bent-Over Row

1. Grab a pair of dumbbells, or if you have your exercise bands, they work great too. Legs should be shoulder width apart, hinging forward at the hips. Keep your core strong and your neck in line with your spine.

2. Bring the weight down toward the floor with the weights facing each other.

3. When you have pulled the weights up to your chest, hold that position for a second. Then, with control, lower the weights down and repeat for indicated number of repetitions.

Step 1:
Begin bent-over row.

Step 2:
Keep your elbows close as you go into the row.

Chest Press

1. Lie back on your physio ball with your hips up, dumbbells in hand, and arms at a 90-degree angle.

2. Position dumbbells to the sides of the upper chest with elbows under dumbbells.

3. Press dumbbells up with elbows to the sides until arms are extended.

4. Lower weight to the sides of the upper chest.

Step 1:
Ready position for chest press.

Step 2:
Raise your arms until they are
straight but do not lock.

 ## Chest Fly

1. Grasp two dumbbells and lie face-up on the physio ball.

2. Support dumbbells above the chest with the arms fixed in a slightly bent position. Rotate shoulders so your elbows are to the sides.

3. Lower dumbbells to the sides until the chest muscles are stretched with elbows fixed.

4. Raise the dumbbells, bringing them together in a hugging motion until dumbbells are nearly together.

Step 1:
Lower your arms.

Step 2:
Hug dumbbells together.

Single-Arm Dumbbell Row

1. Place one foot about two feet in front of the other.

2. With a dumbbell in your left hand, hold your right arm straight on your right knee for support.

3. Keeping your head and chin lifted, pull up the dumbbell until it almost touches your chest.

Make sure you keep your core muscles firmly tight throughout the exercise.

Step 1:
Stabilize your legs and make sure you're balanced.

Step 2:
Pull up dumbbell in one fluid motion.

Military Push-up

1. With your hands on the ground below your shoulders and out about a hand's distance, lower your chest down toward the floor.

2. Keep your elbows away from your body and then press back up into your original position.

Step 1:
Lower your chest to floor.

Step 2:
Raise your body into original position.

Superman

1. Rest your abs on a physio ball and plant toes firmly on the ground, with your legs spread wide to keep your balance. Raise your arms out in front of you in a Y formation.

2. Lift your chest off the ball and lower.

3. You can also rest your hands on your hips while doing the same body movement.

Step 1: Starting position for Superman.

Step 2: Lower down gently, keeping core tight and firm.

Incline Push-up

1. Place your hands on an incline step or a physio ball.

2. Lower your chest, doing a military push-up.

Step 1:
Keeping your core firm, get in ready position.

Step 2:
Remember to use your legs, pulling up your quads as you lower.

Decline Push-Up

1. Place your feet on a physio ball and do a military push-up.

2. Press back up.

Step 1:
Lower,
keeping
chest to
floor.

Step 2:
Keep core
firm as
you lower
and press
back up.

Circuit Training

Circuit training is an efficient, powerful way of doing a cardio workout while at the same time strengthening your upper and lower body, as well as your core. When you move ahead into Phase Two, you will see how these individual movements are put together to give you an all-over body workout.

⚡ Single-Arm Shoulder Press

Holding both hand weights at shoulder height, press one hand up toward the sky and lower. Repeat on other arm.

Step 1:
Ready position for single-arm shoulder press.

Step 2:
Raise one arm while keeping the other arm bent.

Step 3:
Repeat on other side.

Lateral Raise

1. Grasp both hand weights and rest them at your sides.

2. Lift both extended arms up with palms down, stopping at shoulder height.

3. Lower down to your starting position.

Step 1:
Starting position for lateral raise.

Step 2:
Keep arms at shoulder height.

Front Raise

1. Grasp the dumbbell with both hands in an overhand grip.

2. Raise your arms straight in front of you.

Step 1:
Starting position for front raise.

Step 2:
Keep your core firm as you raise your arms.

Upright Row

1. Hold both weights in front of you, palms facing your body.

2. Raise the weights just below your chin, with elbows flying out.

3. Lower back down to first position.

Step 1:
Starting position for upright rows.

Step 2:
Keep feet planted firmly as you raise your elbows to chin level.

I'm sure everyone has done a bicep curl at one point in their life, and it is a great movement. Here I've offered a few variations to add extra challenge.

Bicep Curl

1. Raise arms to bent elbows.

2. Lower back down.

Make sure to keep your elbows at your sides.

Alternating Bicep Curl

With your weights in hand, your shoulders down and pressing flat into your back, and elbows pressing into your side, curl the weight up.

Step 1:
Starting position for alternating bicep curl.

Step 2:
Curl weight up.

NOW FOR THE FUN PART

Do all of this while standing on one foot or on a Bosu ball. You will see that standing on one foot or on an unstable surface will take this effective arm movement and add a different twist to it by using your core strength. You can also add a further challenge by adding pulses forward and up to your alternating bicep curl.

Overhead Tricep Extension

When you are doing an overhead tricep extension, your arms are directly over your head, with your elbows placed on each side of your head. From here the only movement comes from the elbow down to the hand.

1. Drop your hands behind your head at a 90-degree angle and then extend back up to the original position.

2. Raise your arms over your head.

With proper form and alignment, your triceps should be burning and your core should be getting a little toasty too. You can further increase the challenge of this move by doing it on an unstable surface, standing on one foot or on a Bosu ball.

Step 1:
Focusing on your triceps as your hands drop behind your head.

Step 2:
As you raise the weight over your head, make sure your shoulders are pressed down your back.

Tricep Kickback

1. This is another great tricep-strengthening variation. Start with your knees bent slightly and grasp the weights in both hands.

2. Next, lift your arms so they go straight behind you.

Step 1:
Tricep kickback starting position.

Step 2:
Extend arms back in tricep kickback.

Shoulder Press with Leg Squat

This exercise is a great upper and lower body combination strengthener.

1. Grab your hand weights and stand with your arms in front of you at a 90-degree angle from your body and your feet shoulder width apart.

2. Keeping your hands out in front of you at a 90-degree angle, drop your hips down toward the ground. Keep your body weight on your heels to prevent any stress on your knees and let your legs drop as if you are about to sit in a chair.

3. Now as you begin to straighten the legs back to standing, begin to press the weight overhead, with your palms facing forward and your arms extending up.

4. Then lower the weights back down to a 90-degree angle and begin again by lowering your hips.

Step 1:
Push into your legs as you prepare for shoulder press with leg squat.

Step 2:
Keep your shoulders down your back as you push into your legs and raise your arms upward.

Single-Arm Twisting Overhead Press with Squat

This is the same movement as the shoulder press with squat, but you are using one weight.

1. Get into squat position and, with weight in left hand, lower it diagonally across your chest to touch floor next to right foot.

2. Twist your torso as you press into your legs.

3. Stand back up.

4. Raise your weight toward the sky.

Step 1:
The twist comes from your lower ab muscles, not your lower back.

Step 2:
Stand firmly into your legs as you come up.

Step 3:
Make sure you don't lock your elbow when you straighten your arm.

Core Workout

Your core consists of the abdominal muscles that line your upper and lower abdomen and wrap around your lower back. A tight, strong core is essential for all-over body fitness.

Romanian Dead Lift

1. Stand with one weight in both hands and knees slightly bent, with your back straight and core strong.

2. Now, lower your weight down until your body is at a 90-degree angle with the floor.

3. For a little more core strength and balance technique, as you lower your weight down, extend one leg out behind you to form a T with your body.

Step 1:
Starting position for Romanian dead lift.

Step 2:
Pull into your core as you maintain your balance.

Wood Chop

This exercise is a powerful movement similar to a trunk rotation but with a hand weight and a split stance.

1. Stand with your feet wider than hip width apart.

2. Grasp one dumbbell with your right hand.

3. Move your right arm slowly across your body at a diagonal.

4. Lower weight across chest to floor on opposite side.

Step 1:
The wood chop is a slow deliberate movement.

Step 2:
Sink into your legs as you cross and come back.

Horizontal Wood Chop

1. Place both feet forward about four feet apart.

2. Hold one weight with both hands, arms extended.

3. Twist your torso while your hips and feet stay facing front.

4. Repeat motion on other side.

Step 1:
The movement takes the weight from one side of the body to the other.

Step 2:
Keep your hips facing front as you twist your upper body.

Alternating Lunge with Trunk Rotation

1. Holding a weight in both hands, step forward on your right foot, sinking the left knee down toward the floor, making sure to keep your right knee directly over your right heel.

2. Gently twist in the direction of your raised knee.

3. Bring the right foot back to the starting position and proceed to the other side and repeat the motion.

Step 1:
Lunge with weight in both hands.

Step 2:
Twist gently from your upper body, keeping your hips stable.

Step 3:
Starting position for alternating lunge with twist.

Plank Variations

From plank position, there are many core-strengthening movements you can do.

Classic Plank

Place your elbows on the floor, directly under your shoulders, with knees off the ground.

Plank position.

Plank Press on Physio Ball

Press elbows into ball as you raise your chest.

The physio ball challenges you in the plank position.

Push-up on Ball

1. As you press into the ball, make sure your feet are planted firmly.

2. Press all the way until your arms are straight, without locking your elbows.

Step 1:
Extend back into your legs as you push up on the ball.

Step 2:
Tighten your core as you hold the push position.

Uneven Push-Up

1. This push-up requires even more core strength to balance and do the movement.

2. Lower your body, maintaining core strength to help your balance.

Step 1:
Press into ball as you press firmly into your legs.

Step 2:
Lower into uneven push-up.

Plyo Push-up

1. This push-up variation is a challenging move that works core and legs to the max.

2. Keep core firm and tight and use leg strength as you press into floor.

3. Push up.

Step 1:
Jump into low push-up.

Step 2:
Press into floor.

Step 3:
Plyo push-up return.

Walk the Plank

This is the ultimate plank variation.

1. Lean into your elbows, keeping your hands together.

2. Lift one leg at a time.

3. Lower leg and lift other leg.

Step 1:
Starting position for walk the plank.

Step 2:
Push into your standing leg as you lift one leg.

Step 3:
Make sure you use your core here.

Hand Walk

1. Stand upright with your feet about shoulder width apart.

2. Hinge at the hips and place your hands on the ground.

3. Proceed to walk your hands out.

4. Go as far as you can.

5. Hold that position for a couple of seconds and then walk the hands back to your feet and stand up, keeping abdominals strong.

Step 1:
Starting position for hand walk.

Step 2:
Bend toward your toes.

Step 3:
Move gradually, pulling in your core muscles.

Step 4:
Engage your core strength and
hold position before walking back.

Crunches are an intense way to strengthen and tighten your upper and lower abdominal muscles, the heart of your core. Consider these variations.

Ab Crunch on Ball

Put your hands behind your head, supporting your neck and lower back on the ball with feet planted firmly on the ground. Lift chest up to the sky and lower back down to starting position.

Step 1:
Press midback into ball as you lift chest.

Step 2:
Try not to overarch your back as you lower back onto ball.

Side-to-Side Ab Crunch

Same position as above, but this time lift the opposite elbow toward the opposite knee, focusing on obliques.

Step 1:
Keep your midback pressing into the ball as you twist.

Step 2:
Twist to the other side and repeat.

Weighted Crunch

Instead of your hands supporting your neck, grab a hand weight and hold it with both hands. Next, lower weight toward your chest.

Step 1:
Maintain core strength as you raise weight above your head.

Step 2:
The movement comes from the core.

Bicycle Leg Crunch

Lying on your mat, support your neck with your hands and bring your chest up, engaging your core. Then bring your right elbow to your left knee, extending your right leg. Then switch sides and repeat.

Step 1:
Core strengthener with a twist.

Step 2:
Twist to the other side.

Standing Crunch

Standing with your legs about three feet apart, bring your right knee across your body as you bring your left elbow to meet that knee. Next, stand upright with elbows at back of neck. Repeat on other side.

Step 1:
Engage your core strength as you lift leg and twist.

Step 2:
Starting position for standing crunch.

Step 3:
Twist to the other side.

Reverse Ab Crunch

Lie on your back with your legs at a 90-degree angle. Bring both knees up toward your chest. Then raise legs to a 90-degree angle.

Step 1:
Starting position, reverse ab crunch.

Step 2:
Press your arms into floor as you lower knees.

Side Plank

1. Lie on your side with your left leg directly on top of your right.

2. Keeping your feet flexed, lift yourself on your right elbow, extending into your legs. You can keep your left arm in front of you for balance.

3. Lower back down to starting position.

4. Switch sides.

Step 1:
Starting position for side plank.

Step 2:
Lift your midsection toward the ceiling.

Lower-Body Conditioning

When you improve your lower-body strength, you will feel and see the results in many ways, especially during cardio workouts. Your leg muscles and glutes are powerful and large, so their impact on your overall condition is enormous.

Alternating Split Lunge

This movement really works your lower body, especially your hamstrings and glutes. When you add in the repetitions, it also becomes a cardio workout. This is a great way to get your heart rate up and calories burning.

1. Standing upright, take a big step forward with your right foot, knees and toes pointing forward.

2. Drop the back knee down, as close to the ground as you can, without touching it.

3. With your shoulders dropped and flat against your back and your core tight, propel your body weight up as you change your foot position to the other side.

4. Repeat on other side.

Remember to get that back knee down so your front knee is just over your front foot. Placement is everything in this movement, so start off slowly and make sure your knee and foot are in alignment. The more comfortable you are with this, the more you can increase the tempo of the movement.

Step 1:
Starting position for alternating split lunges.

Step 2:
Keep your knee over your foot for proper positioning.

Step 3:
Keep your weight in the center of your body as you press into both legs.

Step 4:
Alternating split lunges.

Squats work your quads and your glutes. Take a look at these powerful variations.

Basic Squat

Sink your weight into your heels as you press down into your legs. Next, push into floor to come to an upright position.

Step 1:
Maintain your balance by keeping your arms folded and in front of you.

Step 2:
Be careful not to hyperextend your knees when you stand up.

Elevated One-Leg Squat

Place your right foot on a step as you lower the left foot down toward the ground. Next, straighten the right leg when the left foot touches the ground.

Step 1:
Keep your right knee in line with your right foot to eliminate any unnecessary stress on the knee.

Step 2:
Rise onto the step with a straight leg.

Sumo Squat

Spread your legs four to five feet apart, with toes pointed out slightly, holding on to one weight. Next, lower the weight down to the floor, keeping your chest up and knees bent. Then take yourself back to the original position.

Step 1:
Assume sumo position.

Step 2:
Starting position for sumo squat.

Weighted Squat

Place legs shoulder width apart and hold two dumbbells. Next, lower your hips down to a 90-degree angle, as if you were about to sit in a chair. Then let your arms hang to your sides and stand back up to the starting position.

Step 1:
Lower your hips.

Step 2:
Starting position for weighted squats.

Bulgarian Split Squat

This is the same movement as a regular lunge, except your back foot is elevated on a step.

Step 1:
Be careful to keep your knee above your ankle as you bend.

Step 2:
Stand up, pressing carefully into front and back legs.

This squat is a repetitive, high-intensity cardio movement that works your lower body while also conditioning you aerobically.

Legs are shoulder width apart with toes forward, hands behind the head. Remember to keep your body weight in your heels to eliminate stress on the knees. The key word here is *speed.* You want to keep a strong pace not only so that you will work all the muscles in your lower body but also so that you get a cardio/fat-burning benefit.

Single Leg Lunge

1. Stand with your feet approximately 3 feet apart.

2. Lower your right knee and raise it back up.

3. Repeat (as indicated) and switch sides.

Step 1:
Starting position, single leg lunge.

Step 2:
Raise your leg carefully and smoothly.

Squat Thrust

1. Stand with your feet about shoulder width apart.

2. Squat down to the floor with your hands on either side of your body.

3. Thrust your legs back into a push-up position.

4. Jump your feet back into a squatting position.

5. Stand up.

Step 1:
Starting position for squat thrusts.

Step 2:
If you can't reach the floor, go as low as possible while maintaining your balance.

Step 3:
Jump back into plank.

Step 4:
Keep chest close to quads.

Step 5:
Resume starting position.

 ## JUMP SQUATS

This is a powerful variation of the squat, adding an intense cardio component.

Mountain Climber

1. Drop down into a push-up position, with your hands directly in alignment with your shoulders. You will immediately feel your whole body has to work to keep you in this position, but no rest for the weary— now you have to add movement!

2. Bring the left knee into your chest and keep your left foot off the ground.

3. Then switch feet.

Keep your momentum going and you will get a great cardio workout while you utilize all of your upper- and lower-body strength.

Step 1:
Keep your right foot firmly planted on the floor.

Step 2:
Move into both legs and your core as you switch.

Reverse Hyperextension on Ball

1. Resting your elbows on the floor and your torso on the ball, place your feet on the ground with legs spread.

2. Lift your legs as your upper body stays firm. Bring your heels together, contracting your lower back. Lower back down.

Step 1:
Starting position for reverse hyperextension.

Step 2:
Maintain your balance by pressing your torso into ball.

Side-to-Side Jump

1. Bend into your knees with your hands together in front of you.

2. From here, with your toes and knees facing forward, jump to the right side.

3. Land with your knees slightly bent on the other side.

Step 1:
Starting position, side-to-side jumps.

Step 2:
Jump to the side.

Step 3:
Land lightly into bent knees.

Sit and Stand

1. Find a step or low chair and sit down.

2. Stand back up.

This is a lot tougher than it sounds!

Step 1:
Lower yourself onto chair or step.

Step 2:
Starting position for sit and stand.

Stretch and Yoga Cool-Down

I always tell my clients that stretching is the fountain of youth—you're only as old as your spine is young. My point? After you've burned some muscle, you need to let those muscles stretch out so they remain supple. Sure, you may still feel sore in a couple of hours—but sore is good, right? You also need to give your body a rest. And that's what this cool-down is all about. As you will see, I suggest about five to eight minutes to stretch and cool down after a workout, using a combination of the stretches described below.

Warrior One

1. Separate your legs about four or five feet apart, with your back leg turned in slightly, your front leg bent in a right angle with the floor. Make sure your knee is in line with your ankle.

2. Raise your arms above your head and sink into your front, bent leg.

Warrior Two

1. From Warrior One, open your arms, allowing your chest to turn away from the forward, bent leg.

2. Keeping your buttocks under your hips, sink into your legs.

Triangle Pose

1. From Warrior Two, straighten your front leg.

2. Standing with your legs about three to four feet apart, keep your left foot pointed forward as the right foot faces out toward the side.

3. Keeping your knees slightly bent and your core strong, extend both arms out to each side of the room and then slowly lower the right arm down toward your knee, chin, or ankle.

4. Raise your left arm toward the ceiling.

5. Gaze toward your left hand unless you feel a strain in your neck. If you do feel a strain in your neck, look down at your right hand. From here you can reach the left arm over your head to get a little more stretch in your rib cage. Repeat to the other side.

6. Try to hold the pose for at least fifteen seconds, and strive for ninety seconds. This is a great overall body stretch and also forces you to use your balance.

Deep Runner's Stretch

This is a great stretch that warms up your hamstrings.

1. From a push-up position, place your right foot directly in between your hands, your knee in line with your foot

2. Then bring your hands on top of the right leg, just above the knee.

3. Repeat on the other side.

Hamstring Stretch

1. Out of your runner's stretch (above), drive your hips high to the ceiling, keeping your hands on the floor.

2. Next, straighten your legs gently and pull your toes up your front leg, toward your chin.

It is important that you keep a slight bend in your knees so you are not putting unnecessary strain on your knees. You are going to feel a great stretch in the backs of your legs, and when you lift your toes the stretch will move into your calves.

Quad Stretch

1. Stand upright, with shoulders back and down and core strength strong.

2. Bring the heel of your right foot up toward your hamstrings/glutes and hold with the same arm.

3. Switch sides.

If your balance is challenged in this movement, you can always use a chair or a nearby wall to keep your balance. However, play around with your balance, too, because the better your balance, the greater your abdominal strength. Don't forget to do the other side. You can always reach the opposite hand up toward the ceiling for balance supreme!

 Calf Stretch

1. Stand on a stair or on the edge of a step.

2. Move one foot back toward the edge of the stair, so that only your toes are touching the edge.

3. Lower your heel toward the ground until you feel a good stretch in your calf.

4. Hold for fifteen to thirty seconds.

5. Repeat with your other leg.

Seated Pike Stretch

1. Have a seat on your mat with your legs extended in front of you and your big toes together.

2. Reach your arms as high as you can up toward the ceiling and then slowly lower your chest down to your quads. If you need to grab a towel to place on the bottom of your feet and grab the towel, feel free.

3. Take big deep breaths into your hamstrings and release your body, letting it go where it feels comfortable.

Don't ever push your body past the point of a good stretch to a dangerous area where you run the risk of injury. Take your time and relax.

From seated pike, bend one leg in toward the other, so foot meets straight leg at angle. Gently bend forward toward the foot of your straight leg.

Sit on floor or mat and place feet together, forming a triangle with your legs, letting your muscles release.

Glute Stretch

Lying on your back, extend one leg, resting it on the floor. Pull the other knee into your chest. You can add a twist to the opposite side to get a nice stretch across your lower back.

Seated Dancer Stretch

1. Sit on your mat with your legs extended out to each side.

2. From here, reach high to the ceiling and then slowly lower the torso down and place your hands down on the floor.

Take your time with this stretch. You will definitely feel this through your inner thighs and up through your spine and neck.

Downward Dog

1. Get onto your hands and knees, setting your knees directly below your hips and your hands slightly forward of your shoulders.

2. Spread your fingers and push into your legs. At first keep the knees slightly bent and the heels lifted away from the floor.

3. Then lift your "sit bones" toward the ceiling and gently straighten your knees without locking them.

4. Keep your arms firm and press your shoulder blades down your back.

Upward Dog

1. Lie on the floor, stretching your legs back, with the tops of your feet on the floor.

2. Bend your elbows and spread your palms on the floor beside your waist so that your forearms are relatively perpendicular to the floor.

3. Straighten your arms and lift your chest so that your belly button comes off the floor.

4. Then lift the weight off your thighs as you look up toward the ceiling.

I have saved the best for last.

1. Have a seat on your mat in a comfortable cross-legged position, with your hands resting in your lap and your shoulders down and back.

2. Keeping your core firm and your eyes closed, sit at peace for at least a minute.

Think of this cool-down as a gift to your body and mind. Just as it's important to warm up your body before working out, it's equally important to quiet and cool down your body with some stretching and breathing. This not only helps your body relax and rest after an intense workout but also enables your mind to come to a peaceful place. Namaste.

Before long, all of these exercises in my master list will be familiar, but as you move forward and begin Phase Two of your workout, you can always refer to this list when you need to be reminded of correct positioning and make adjustments to increase (or lower) intensity.

TEN

The Workout

— Phase Two —

How alive do you feel? How amazing is it to experience your body as real, physical energy moving through space? Does your brain also feel clearer? Your step lighter? Your skin softer and smoother?

As you move into Phase Two, adding strength training of your upper body, lower body, and core to your cardio workout, you will experience these wonderful benefits—and then some. Pure cardio got your heart pumping, but strength training will make your heart even stronger. You will not only intensify your weight loss by building lean muscle mass, you will transform your silhouette.

But always remember one of the core (no pun intended) principles from your Inner Compass work: When you reconnect with your body and make this commitment to take care of yourself, you literally transform who you are in the world. So yes, your body is going to change—you will look better in the mirror. But the most important transformation is when that click happens on the inside. Once you truly understand how and why you are taking care of your body, the world becomes your oyster.

So as you try out these three workout options I've created, keep in mind that each action is an expression of you taking care of yourself. Be mindful. Be patient. Give yourself time to learn these workouts gradually. You will get to a place where you can do them more efficiently and with more mastery. But it's not a race. It's all about the journey.

Now let's move!

The Big Picture

Phase Two consists of four components that you will be doing for forty-five to sixty minutes, five days a week.

1. *Warm-up of five minutes.* This is essentially a five-minute walk on a treadmill or any other activity that gets your heart pumping and your mind focused on your workout. I like to think of the warm-up as the light switch that turns on my brain to exercise.

2. *Cardio.* You will be doing exclusively cardio on two days each week. As you did in Phase One's pure cardio workout, you have the choice to either walk or investigate other options, including spinning, cycling, swimming, or step class—essentially any exercise that trains you aerobically.

3. *Circuit training.* On the three remaining days, you will be doing a workout of forty-five to sixty minutes that focuses on strengthening combinations of upper body, lower body, and/or core muscles (your abdominal muscles). Because of the emphasis on repetitions, these strength-training exercises become a cardio workout as well.

4. *Core challenge.* One day a week you will do a workout that focuses primarily on strengthening your core muscles (those that wrap around your middle, including your abdominals and lower back), while also exercising other larger muscle groups in your upper and lower body. Again, these core challenge routines also comprise a cardio workout through repetitions.

During Phase Two you will have three different workout options (see below) to follow. I offer adjustments to make the workout easier or more difficult, and I also offer a range of repetitions that alters the intensity of the workout. As you become familiar with the individual exercises, your confidence, strength, and agility will increase.

You can also use the master list to create your own combinations and routines by choosing from the four categories. But if you design your own workout, remember to vary the muscle groups: upper body, lower body, and core.

I always recommend that people begin using the lowest amount of free weights (3 or 5 pounds). As you become more comfortable and confident, you will naturally want to increase the weights. You can always check your perceived degree of exertion to make sure you stay in the "challenge" zone that's right for you.

Workout Option One

Monday

1. Warm-up: 5-minute walk on treadmill, level 1–2 incline

2. Stretch: trunk rotation, side-to-side lunges, floor back extensions

3. Circuit training

    - Push-up/Pull-up, 12–15 reps

    - Incline dumbbell press on your physio ball using a 10–15-pound dumbbell, 12–15 reps

    - Bent-over row, using the same weights for 12–15 reps

    - Split Lunge, 10–15 reps. Although this is a great squat strengthener, it also works the core and the glutes.

    - Ab crunch on the physio ball, 20–25 reps. Repeat the circuit 3 times.

4. Cool-down. The cool-down should last at least five minutes and can be made up of any number or combinations of stretches (refer to the Stretch and Yoga cool-down, pages 194–214) to help bring your body back to a restful state.

Tuesday

1. Warm-up

2. Cardio

3. Cool-down

Wednesday

1. Warm-up

2. Circuit training

   - Single-arm shoulder press, using 5–10-pound weights, 12–15 reps

   - Upright row, same weights, 12–15 reps

   - Front raise, same weights, 12–15 reps

   - Alternating bicep curl, same weights, 12–15 reps

   - Overhead tricep extension, same weights, 12–15 reps

   - Elevated one-leg squat, 10–15 reps on each leg

   - Sumo squat, 15–20 reps.

   Repeat this circuit 3 times.

3. Cool-down

Thursday

1. Warm-up

2. Cardio

3. Cool-down

Friday

1. Warm-up

2. Core challenge

   - Single-leg Romanian dead lift, using 10-pound weights, 12–15 reps on each leg

   - Wood chop, using 5–10-pound weights, 12–15 reps on each side

   - Alternating lunge, holding 1–5-pound weights, with a trunk rotation, 10 reps each leg

   - Plank press on physio ball, hold for as long as you can, up to 30 seconds

   - Push-up on the physio ball, 5–10 reps

   - Twist trunk rotation on the physio ball, 15 reps.

   Repeat circuit 3 times.

3. Cool-down

Workout Option Two

Monday

1. Warm-up

2. Circuit training

   - Chest press on bench, using 10–15-pound weights, 12–15 reps

   - Chest fly, using same weights, 12–15 reps

   - Single-arm dumbbell row, using same weights, 12–15 reps on each arm

   - Weighted squat, rest the same weights on your shoulders, 15 reps

   - Side-to-side ab crunch, 15–20 reps

- Military push-up, 10 reps

- Superman (back extension) on a mat or a ball, 15 reps.

Repeat circuit 3 times.

3. Cool-down

Tuesday

1. Warm-up

2. Cardio

3. Cool-down

Wednesday

1. Warm-up

2. Stretch

3. Circuit training

- Shoulder press with leg squat, using 8–12-pound weights, 12–15 reps

- Side raise on one leg, using 5–8-pound weights, 8 reps on each leg

- Alternating hammer curl, using the same weights, 10 reps on each arm

- Tricep kickback, same weights, 12–15 reps on each arm

- Jump squat, 10–15 reps

- Standing weighted side crunch, using same weights, 15 reps on each side.

Repeat circuit 3 times.

4. Cool-down

Thursday

1. Warm-up

2. Cardio

3. Cool-down

Friday

1. Warm-up

2. Core challenge

   • Hand walk, 15 reps

   • Uneven push-up, 5–8 reps on each arm

   • Speed squat, time yourself for 30–45 seconds

   • Weighted crunch, using 10-pound weights, 12–15 reps

   • Bent-over row, using 10-pound weights, 12–15 reps

   • Jump squat, go for 30–45 seconds.

   Repeat circuit 3 times.

Workout Option Three

Monday

1. Warm-up

2. Circuit training

   • Incline push-up, 8 reps

   • Flat push-up, 8 reps

   • Decline push-up, 8 reps

   • Push-up/pull-up

- Single-leg lunge with 5–10-pound weights or without weights, 10–12 reps on each leg

- Bicycle leg crunch, go for 30–45 seconds

- Push-up, 10 reps

- Dead lift, using 10-pound weights, 12–15 reps

- Standing crunch, alternating elbow/knee, 15 reps on each side.

Repeat circuit 3 times.

3. Cool-down

Tuesday

1. Warm-up

2. Cardio

3. Stretch

Wednesday

1. Warm-up

2. Circuit training

- One-arm twisting overhead press with a squat, using 8–10-pound weights, 10 reps on each side

- Bicep curl, using rubber band, 12–15 reps

- Tricep extension with rubber bands, 15–20 reps

- Rubber band squat, 15 reps

- Overhead press with bands, 15–20 reps

- Lower abdominals crunch, 15–20 reps.

Repeat circuit 3 times.

3. Cool-down

Thursday

1. Warm-up

2. Cardio

3. Cool-down

Friday

1. Warm-up

2. Overall body conditioning

   • Jumping jack, 15–20 reps

   • Plyo push-up, 8–10 reps

   • Squat thrust, 15 reps

   • Hamstring curl using physio ball, 15 reps

   • Ab crunch with legs on the ball, add lower abs by pulling your knees into elbows, 15 reps

   • Mountain climber, 15 reps

   • Plank pose with one arm, hold 15 seconds on each arm.

   Repeat workout 3 times.

Adding Intensity

You can always intensify any one of the three workouts in three ways: You increase the number of repetitions, you increase the weight, or you can lengthen the time for an individual exercise. This is no joke! You will soon learn to put the hammer down and come to a whole new level of you.

You can also extend your workout to 60–75 minutes. And if you are really feeling exhilarated by this extra level of intensity, you may want to add one more day of cardio. All of the combinations are fat-burning circuits that will definitely put your body to the test.

This outer strengthening also has an inner result: Your mind will feel clearer, and your ability to focus will become greater. Building up your strength will make your confidence and motivation soar!

Parting Words

I hope with all my heart that you let the power of the Inner Compass plan, as well as my eating and fitness plans, show you a path to true health and well-being. Getting healthy, fit, and strong is a choice all of us can make. It's a decision that requires commitment, will, and a lot of faith that what sometimes may feel like an insurmountable task becomes not only realistic but a job well done.

And remember, taking care of yourself does not happen in four weeks, eight weeks, or twelve weeks. It's a lifestyle, not a plan.

I wish you luck, health, and happiness!